colorwork for Adventurous knitters

Master the Art of Knitting **Stripes**, **Slipstitch**, **Intarsia**, and **Stranded Colorwork**
through Step-by-Step Instruction and Easy Projects

Lori Ihnen

I dedicate this book to Kevin and Christina

Acknowledgments

I would like to thank the following yarn companies for supplying me with beautiful fibers: Berroco Yarns, Blue Sky Alpacas, Brown Sheep Company, Frog Tree Yarns, Louet North America, Rauma Yarns, Russi Sales, and Shibui Knits. An extra thank you goes to Louet North America for the yarn used in all the samplers.

I would also like to thank the following knitters for their skill and help to make this book a reality: Mary Brown, Anne C. Jones, Kristine King, Karen B. Lehman, Jane Niemi, and Elizabeth Watkins.

And finally thank you to Karen Weiberg for her expertise and technical editing and to the staff at Creative Publishing international for all their hard work.

colorwork for
Adventurous
knitters

Master the Art of Knitting Stripes,
Slipstitch, Intarsia, and Stranded Colorwork
through Step-by-Step Instruction
and Easy Projects

Lori Ihnen

Creative Publishing
international

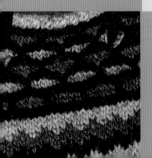

First published in the United States of America by Creative Publishing international, Inc., a member of Quayside Publishing Group

400 First Avenue North, Suite 300

Minneapolis, MN 55401

1-800-328-3895

www.creativepub.com or www.Qbookshop.com

Visit www.Craftside.Typepad.com for a behind-the-scenes peek at our crafty world!

ISBN: 978-1-58923-706-3

Printed in China

10 9 8 7 6 5 4 3 2 1

Library of Congress Cataloging-in-Publication Data

Ihnen, Lori, 1962-

Colorwork for adventurous knitters / Lori Ihnen.

    p. cm.

Summary: "Technique reference for advanced beginner level knitting skills that incorporate multiple colors into the knitted fabric. Includes complete instructions for fifteen projects"— Provided by publisher.

ISBN 978-1-58923-706-3 (spiral bound)

1. Knitting. 2. Knitting—Pattern. 3. Color in art. I. Title.

TT820.I385 2012

746.43'2—dc23

         2012010570

Technical/Copy Editor: Karen Weiberg

Proofreader: Karen Ruth

Design, layout and charts: Diana Boger

Photographer: Corean Komarec

Photo Stylist: Joanne Wawra

Contents

Introduction

When you think of colorwork, do you cringe or do you get excited? Within the chapters of this book there is a wealth of information on colorwork in its simplest form to its most challenging.

Each of the sections in this book explores a different category of colorwork. Within each section you will find techniques, pattern samples, and projects. The pattern samples highlight techniques just learned; some are classic patterns and others are originals. This book is not meant as a stitch library, but the samples provided will give good practice for the techniques. The projects continue to build on newly learned skills with smaller but attractive designs.

The first section—Stripes—is the most basic and from there each section gets a little bit more complicated. You can read the sections separately and out of order, but some techniques do build from what is learned in the previous sections. For example, in the stripes section jog fixes are a main focus, and these same issues can come up again with stranded knitting and patterns that are in color bands.

It's assumed that you have basic knitting skills and know how to knit, purl, increase, and decrease. Because there are many charts, **here is a quick overview on how to read charts.** Each square represents a color to be knit and the color changes that will occur. **To read a chart for back and forth knitting,** start at the bottom right corner. This is the right side of your knitting and you will read the chart from right to left. When you get to the end of this row and turn your work, you will be on the wrong side of your knitting, so you will read the chart from left to right. **If you are working in the round** you will always read the chart from right to left, every round.

At the end of the book there is a section called Knitting Techniques. You will find cast-ons, three-needle bind off, I-cord, twisted cord, and a few good tips, so check that out. Some patterns will reference these techniques too.

In practicing a new technique, use a high quality fiber and a larger gauge yarn. Remember to always check your gauge as you begin a new project. To get the best results, use the yarn suggested in the pattern. If you substitute yarns, choose a similar fiber and swatch, swatch, swatch. If your gauge does not match the pattern gauge, adjust your needles up or down until you have the correct stitch gauge. Remember to treat your gauge swatch as you would your garment. Block and launder to save disappointment, otherwise when you launder your garment for the first time, it could grow or shrink.

This book is about enhancing your colorwork skills, making your colorwork experience more fun and pleasurable, making you more confident, and expanding your colorwork experiences. Let's get started!

STRIPES

A fun, exciting, and simple way to add color to
your knitting is to use stripes. Stripes can be as simple as a
two color repeat or as complex as changing colors every row.
Stripes can be made in stockinette stitch or in patterned
stitches, the choice is up to you.

Techniques

Although striping seems pretty straightforward—changing yarn colors between rows or rounds—there are methods and tricks to perfect those color changes and to make them as inconspicuous as possible. Striping techniques for knitting back and forth on two needles are different from those used when knitting circularly. There are advantages and disadvantages to both. How you make the color changes and what you do with the yarn when it's not in use make a big difference in the quality of the finished fabric.

CHANGING COLORS WHEN WORKING FLAT

When working back and forth in rows, there are a few things to master when it comes to changing colors.

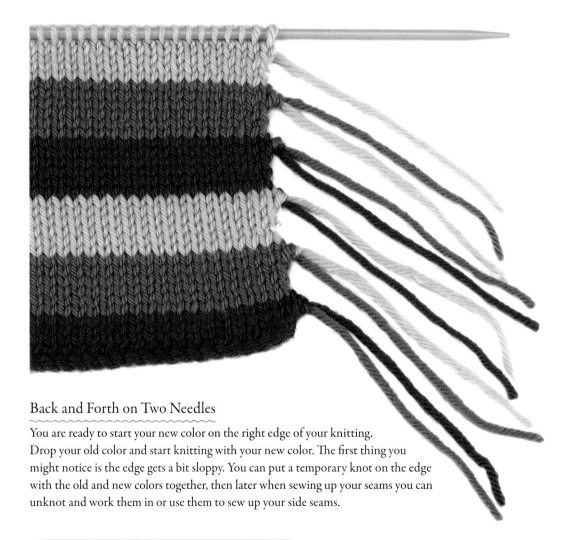

Back and Forth on Two Needles

You are ready to start your new color on the right edge of your knitting. Drop your old color and start knitting with your new color. The first thing you might notice is the edge gets a bit sloppy. You can put a temporary knot on the edge with the old and new colors together, then later when sewing up your seams you can unknot and work them in or use them to sew up your side seams.

Carry Yarn

If you were to cut each time you changed colors, you would have many ends to deal with. A neater finish is to carry your yarn up the edge. When carrying up the edge, be careful not to pull up too tightly or the edge of your knitting will pucker and be shorter and less elastic. Carry yarns about three or four rows. If the stripe is wider than that, either cut the yarn or catch the carried yarn with your working yarn at the edge. This can be done by twisting the carried yarn; to do this at the edge, lift the carried yarn up and over the working yarn and knit the edge stitch. This will lock it into the edge.

▲ Locking the edge: The brown yarn is dropped to the right and the next color in the sequence, orange, is picked up from behind. Knit across with orange. Note at the edge the twist that is formed when the colors are locked.

Back and Forth on a Circular Needle

Another way to knit stripes back and forth is to use a circular needle to knit back and forth as if you were using straight needles. Sometimes your stripe sequence will end at the opposite side of where you just ended working your row. Since you are on a circular needle, all you need to do is to slide your stitches along the cable and begin knitting again from the other end of your needle. This is especially easy if you are working stockinette stitch (knit on the right side and purl on the wrong side) and works great if you are working an odd number of rows.

▼ Notice that the row just finished is white and has ended on the left. If you were to continue knitting with white, you would turn your knitting and purl across the back. But the next row of pattern is warm brown and that color ended at the opposite side. Since you are working on circular needles, slide the work to the other end of the needle and knit across with warm brown.

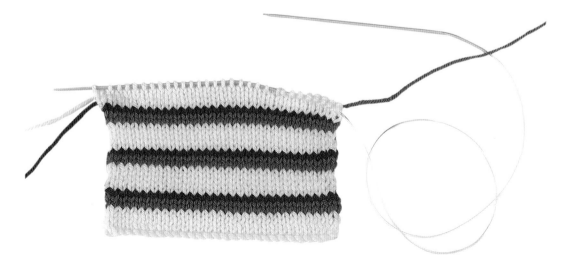

CIRCULAR KNITTING

The advantages of knitting in the round are color changes all occur at the starting point of the rounds, and if it's a garment, there are no side seams to sew. The disadvantage is at the start point you will get a jog in your knitting when changing colors. When you knit back and forth, each row is completed and the next row is directly above it. When you knit circularly, you are making a spiral, so the ends of the rounds don't meet but rather continue one stitch higher. There are a few techniques to minimize the jog. If the jog occurs at the side seam of a garment sometimes it is easiest to ignore it. Decide how much the jog offends you. If you are using finer yarn the jog will be less noticeable compared to a bulkier yarn.

▲ Jog that occurs in circular knitting.

These notes refer to all jog fixes:

Note: All jog fix instructions use a marker for reference to the actions taken, always marking the beginning of the round.

Note: Because color changes are all happening on top of each other, there will be loose yarns on the wrong side of the fabric and it will look sloppy. When all your yarns are worked in and finished off, the area will neaten.

Jog Fix #1

This fix needs two or more rounds to use.

▲ Jog Fix #1.
The lifted and first stitch knit together highlighted.

1. Work one row of new color, slip marker. Lift the back of the stitch from the row below and place on left-hand needle.

2. Knit the first and lifted stitch together.

The disadvantage to this technique is the beginning of each round is one stitch height shorter than the rest. This is only a problem if there are many stripes because losing a stitch height at this point repeatedly, can cause the fabric to draw down or pucker over a larger area. This is a nice fix to use if your stripes are further apart and happen less frequently.

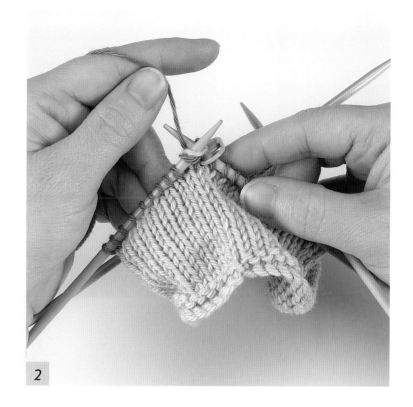

Jog Fix #2

1. *Work one round of new color. At the start of the next round, remove the marker from the needle, slip the first stitch, and replace the marker after the slip stitch.
2. Knit desired rounds. Repeat from *.

The advantage to this fix is all the rows stay the same height. The disadvantage is with every color change the start of the row moves over one to the left. This can cause a slight spiral, and if you have many stripes, the start point could move to an undesirable area, such as the front of a hat.

▲ Jog Fix #2.
Slip stitch highlighted.

Jog Fix #3

This jog fix is the same as Jog Fix #2 except do not move your marker one to the left.

The advantage of this fix is the color change remains in the same place. The disadvantage is similar to Jog Fix #1, you lose one row on that first slipped stitch and the fabric will draw down slightly. If you have many stripes, this could shorten or pucker at this point.

▲ Jog Fix #3.
Slip stitch highlighted.

Jog Fix #4

I discovered this fix, and made up my own variation, similar to Jog Fix #2. As long as the start of your next color change row does not fall on top of the start of the previous color by 2 stitches (or more), you will not form a spiral. In order not to jog, start your color changes at different points on your knitting, forward and backward.

Within your color block area you will have spiraling, but since it's in the same color, you will not see it.

Your marker does not move, but the beginning of your round does. No matter where the first

▲ Jog Fix #4.
The first stitch of each color change is highlighted.

stitch starts, say two stitches after the marker, when the rounds of striping are done, it will need to end two stitches after the marker, thus making a complete round.

1. Knit to the point where you want to change colors, ending at the marker. Slip the marker and the next two stitches. This becomes your new start point, two stitches past the marker.

Note: You could add a second different colored marker to use as you move your beginning points around and keep your original marker to mark your "true" starting point.

2. With new color, knit the required number of rounds, ending at your new start point. (2 sts past the marker).

3. Slip two stitches from right needle back to left needle, you will be back at your marker. The new color can start here at marker or slip the marker and the next two stitches from the right needle back to the left needle and knit the required rounds with the new color at its new starting point.

4. Continue in this manner moving your starting point around. It doesn't matter if you slip 2, 3, or 4 stitches (don't do less than 2), only that you complete your rounds and move your starting points around.

3

If your stripes are narrow and you want to carry the yarns up rather than cut them, you must carry the yarn straight up or to the left. Carrying a yarn to the right will create a small hole.

An advantage to moving two stitches is the start points do not all line up, which makes for easier color changes with all the loose ends not occurring directly on top of each other. The rounds stay the same height and the starts are not on top of each other, making for a bit easier knitting. The disadvantage, as with all fixes, is that you see a slight dip where the colors change, but with this technique the dip is very slight.

STRIPED RIBS

When making ribs with color stripes a dot from the preceding color will show up on your purled stitches. This could be considered a design choice or an untidy dot. If you do not like the dot it is easily eliminated by knitting the first row of the color change, assuming you have three or more rows to your color stripe. Then continue with your ribbing pattern, as in this case a knit two, purl two. This one row of knit (or purl if your color change occurs on the wrong side) will not change your amount of elasticity and will eliminate the dot.

Striped Stitch Patterns

The following five stripe patterns will provide good practice in changing colors. With the aid of the chart, you can convert to knitting in the round by changing the even numbered rows. On the even numbered rows the knits become purls and purls become knits. The first two patterns are easily converted, but the last three are a bit more challenging. Remember to work the opposite; as in the Daisy Stitch, instead of p3tog, it becomes a k3tog.

BASIC STRIPE

Basic stripes can be dramatic. This sample, if knit flat, should still be done on circular needles because the stripe has odd numbered repeats. Some color changes will occur on the opposite side of where your row just ended. Just slide the stitches to the other end of the cable and continuing in stockinette stitch with the new color.

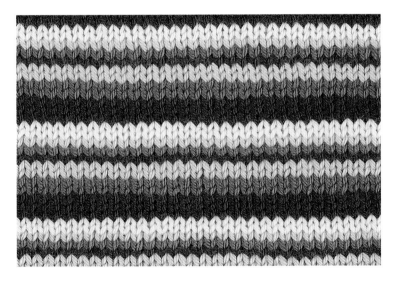

Worked on any number of sts.
Four colors: A, B, C, and D.
Follow chart for color changes.

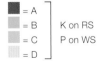

= A
= B   K on RS
= C   P on WS
= D

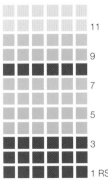

TEXTURED STRIPE

As when making ribs, when you change colors you will need to make one row in knit so you will not have a 'dot' from the previous row. Look closely at the chart, and you can see there is a knit row at each color change. You do not notice this row in the knitted swatch as the purl bumps lay on top of the knit row.

Multiple of 2 sts.
Three colors: A, B, and C.
Follow chart for color changes.

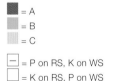

■ = A
■ = B
▥ = C

⊟ = P on RS, K on WS
☐ = K on RS, P on WS

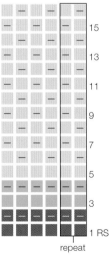

repeat

DAISY STITCH (STAR STITCH)

This cute pattern can be used to make a two-color stripe pattern but can also be used to make stripes with as many color changes as desired. Colors can be changed every two rows.

Multiple of 4 sts plus 1.
Two colors: A and B or three colors;
A, B, and C.

Make star: p3tog leaving sts on needle, yo, p3tog again.

Row 1 (RS): With A, knit.

Row 2: With A, k1, *make star, k1; repeat from * to end.

Row 3: With B, knit.

Row 4: With B, k1, p1, k1, *make star, k1; repeat from *, end p1, k1.

Repeat rows 1-4.

LITTLE CROWNS

This pattern has a similar feel to Daisy Stitch, but incorporates yarn-overs and the (k1, p1, k1) move is made on the right side of the fabric. Garter stitch separates the crown rows.

Multiple of 3 sts plus 2.
Three colors: A, B, and C.

Row 1 (RS): With A, knit.

Row 2: With A, knit.

Row 3: With B, k1, knit to last st wrapping yarn twice around needle for each st, end k1.

Row 4: With B, k1, *slip next 3 sts to RH needle dropping extra loops, slip these 3 sts back to LH needle, k1, p1, k1 through 3 sts tog: repeat from *, end k1.

Rows 5 & 6: Same as rows 1 & 2.

Row 7 & 8: With C, same as rows 3 & 4.

Repeat rows 1-8 for repeat.

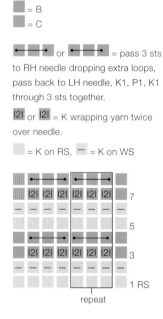

= A

= B

= C

or = pass 3 sts to RH needle dropping extra loops, pass back to LH needle, K1, P1, K1 through 3 sts together.

|2| or |2| = K wrapping yarn twice over needle.

= K on RS, — = K on WS

repeat

GRANITE RELIEF STITCH

Four rows make up each color stripe in this pattern. This swatch uses 4 colors; any number of color changes can be used, as few as 2 or as many colors as you have. Rows will have different row counts because of rapid deceases and increases in rows 2 and 3.

Multiple of 2.
Four colors: A, B, C, and D.

Row 1 (RS): With A knit.

Row 2: With A, k2tog across.

Row 3: With A, k into the front and back of each st.

Row 4: With A, purl.

Repeat these 4 rows changing colors as desired.

V = K into front and back of stitch
Δ = K2 tog WS
= K on RS, P on WS

repeat

Striped Pillow

This pillow is designed using an interesting stripe, knit back and forth. The assembly makes for minimal finishing. The horizontal band is knit first, which includes both the front and back. When the required length is done, it is finished off with a three-needle bind off. Then stitches are picked up along both the front and back edges and the vertical section is knit, again with the edge being finished off with a three-needle bind off. The pillow form is then inserted with only one seam to sew.

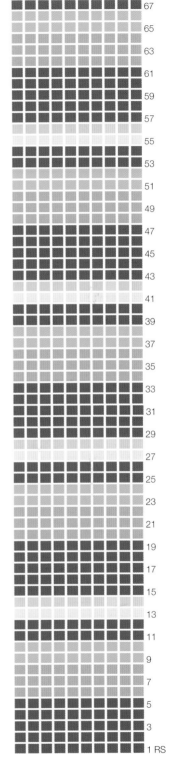

MATERIALS

Medium-weight yarn in 5 colors

1 each Blue Sky Alpaca Worsted Cotton, 100% cotton, 3.5 oz (100 g), 150 yd (137 m): 624 Indigo (A), 632 Mediterranean (B), 633 Pickle (C), 618 Orchid (D), 640 Hyacinth (E)

12" × 16" (30.5 cm × 40.6 cm) pillow form

Size 7 (4.5 mm) 24" (61 cm) circular needles (2 sets or an extra straight needle for 3-needle BO) or size to obtain gauge

Tapestry needle

Gauge

16 sts and 22 rows = 4" (10 cm) in Stockinette Stitch on size 7 (4.5 mm) needles

Finished Measurements

12" × 16" (30.5 × 40.6 cm)

Instructions

With size 7 (4.5 mm) circular needle and A, CO 44 sts.

Working back and forth, follow chart to row 67.

Evenly divide sts onto two needles. With right sides facing, 3-needle BO top edge (page 141).

Next: With circular needle and A, PU 48 sts along the front and 48 sts along the back edges for a total of 96 sts.

Work rows 1–58.

Evenly divide sts onto two needles. With right sides facing, 3-needle BO (page 141) side edge.

Block.

Insert pillow form and sew bottom edge.

Striped Pillow Chart

■ = A
▨ = B
▨ = C
□ = D
▨ = E

Striped Hat

Simple stripes and a cute wavy edge make up this fun hat. The same wavy edge is used to make a flower at the top. I used the technique of Jog Fix #4 as explained on page 14. Candy Apple Red (B) was 2 sts to the left of marker, Burgundy (C) was at the marker, and Crabapple Blossom (A) was 2 sts to the right of the marker.

MATERIALS

1 Each Louet Gems #3 Light/ Light Worsted Weight 100% Merino Wool; 3.5 oz (100 g), 175 yd (160 m) 26 Crabapple Blossom (A), 63 Candy Apple Red (B), and 58 Burgundy (C)

Size 4 (3.5 mm) 16" (41 cm) circular needles or size to gauge

Size 5 (3.75 mm) 16" (41 cm) circular and double pointed needles or size to obtain gauge

Gauge

20 sts and 28 rounds = 4" (10 cm) in Stockinette Stitch with size 5 (3.75 mm) needles

Finished Measurements

Approximately 20" (51 cm) at brim and 7½" (19 cm) long

Instructions

Wavy Edge Pattern (Multiple of 11 sts)

Rounds 1, 2, and 4: Knit.

Round 3: *P2tog twice, (M1, k1) 3 times, M1, p2tog twice, repeat from * to end.

With size 4 (3.5 mm) circular needle and A, Cable CO 110 sts. Join, being careful not to twist. Work one repeat of Wavy Edge Pattern.

With B, knit one round, purl one round.

Next: Work k1, p1 rib for 5 rounds.

Change to size 5 (3.75 mm) circular

needles and C, knit one row.

Next row evenly increase 5 stitches, 115 sts.

Work following chart to row 43.

Then follow decrease instructions below and continue to use chart for color changes. Change to double pointed needles when needed.

Round 43: * K2tog, k3, repeat from * to end. (92 sts).

Rounds 44 & 45: Knit.

Round 46: * K2tog, k2, repeat from * to end. (69 sts).

Round 47: Knit.

Round 48: * K2tog, k1, repeat from * to end. (46 sts).

Round 49: Knit.

Round 50: K2tog across. (23 sts).

Round 51: K2tog across, end k1. (12 sts).

Cut tail and use to thread through loops and close up the hole.

Flower

With size 4 (3.50 mm) needles and A, Cable CO 77 sts. Work Wavy Edge Pattern back and forth as follows:

Row 1: Knit.

Rows 2 & 4: purl.

Row 3: *P2tog twice, (M1, k1) 3 times, M1, p2tog twice, * repeat from * to end.

Cut long tail and thread through loops. Coil into flower and sew to top of hat.

Striped Hat Chart

= A
= B
= C
X = Decrease Rows

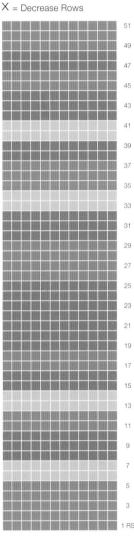

51
49
47
45
43
41
39
37
35
33
31
29
27
25
23
21
19
17
15
13
11
9
7
5
3
1 RS

Striped Zigzag Scarf

A new twist to a traditional pattern, this exciting zigzag scarf is knit with one variegated and four solid colored yarns. The scarf is knit on the long edge, requiring you to cast on a large number of stitches. To make the cast-on easier, add markers every 50 stitches to aid in counting. You must use a circular knitting needle with a long cable to comfortably accommodate all the stitches.

MATERIALS

1 each Staccato Sock, 65% Superwash Merino, 30% Silk, 5% Nylon; 1.75 oz (50 g), 191 yd (175 m), Summer Camp (A), Suit (B), Tide (C), Artichoke (D), and Rain (E)

Size 4 (3.5 mm) 29" (74 cm) circular needles or size to obtain gauge

Gauge

30 sts and 8 rows = 4" (10 cm) in Zigzag pattern on size 4 (3.5 mm) needles

Finished Measurements

5½" (14 cm) wide by 62" (155 cm) long

Row Patterns

RSP (Right Side Purl): k1, ssk *p9, sl 2, k1, p2sso; repeat from *, end p9, k2tog, k1.

RSK (Right Side Knit): k1, ssk *k9, sl 2, k1, p2sso; repeat from *, end k9, k2tog, k1.

WSP (Wrong Side Purl): k1, p5 *(p1, yo, p1 in next st), p9; repeat from *, end (p1, yo, p1 in next st), p5, k1.

Instructions

With B, cable CO 459 sts.

Row 1 (RS): With B, RSP.

Row 2: With C, WSP.

Row 3: With C, RSK.

Row 4: With A. WSP.

Row 5: With A, RSP.

Row 6: With A, WSP.

Row 7: With A, RSP.

Row 8: With A, WSP.

Row 9: With A, RSK.

Row 10: With D, WSP.

Row 11: With D, RSP.

Row 12: With E, WSP.

Row 13: With E, RSK.

Row 14: With B, WSP.

Repeat rows 1-14 two more times (a total of 3 repeats).

End: With B, BO in pattern RSP.

SLIP STITCH & MOSAIC

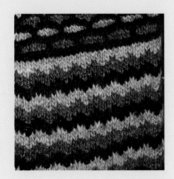

An easy way to add beautiful color to your knitting is to
use slip stitch patterns and mosaic stitch patterns. These patterns
can be very simple to make and are very effective in producing
a lovely ornamented fabric.

Techniques

Looking complicated but easy to execute, slip stitch and mosaic patterns use only one yarn or color per row. They produce a fabric that is dense and is tightly knit because the stitch is pulled up and is knit in the following row or even stretched over several rows. This can make the fabric less elastic, so using a bigger needle can help relax this tendency. A fine or soft yarn is also a good choice for these patterns. The natural tendencies of this type of stitch make them perfect for outerwear like hats, mittens, and jackets. They are also strong, which makes them equally good for purses, bags, and similar items.

SLIP STITCH

There are two main concerns with slipping stitches. The first is which way to insert the needle; purlwise or knitwise. The standard practice is to insert your needle purlwise unless the pattern specifically tells you to do the opposite. This way, the stitch is oriented correctly on the needle, ready to be knit or purled on the next row. If you slip knitwise, your stitch will be twisted. You should slip purlwise whether you are on the right side or wrong side of your work unless your pattern instructs otherwise.

▲ Slipping your stitch purlwise

The second concern is where the working yarn is held, in front as if to purl or in back as if to knit. It could be in either position, all depending on the pattern. So if the instructions do not specify, your yarn will be held toward the wrong side of your fabric. So when working on the right side, your yarn is held behind the needles, also known as "with yarn in back" (abbreviated as wyib). On the wrong side of your work the yarn is held in front of the needles or "with yarn in front" (abbreviated as wyif).

▲ Slipping stitches with yarn in back

▲ Slipping stitches with yarn in front

MOSAIC

Mosaic patterns are made with slip stitches and use one color per two rows. Therefore mosaic patterns change colors on every right side row, so the same colored yarn is always used in two row increments. Mosaic knitting can be either a garter stitch base or stockinette stitch base. Garter stitch mosaics are condensed and the motifs have a framed feel. Stockinette stitch mosaics, while still dense, do not have as thick of an appearance and can look more like stranded knitting. On the stockinette base the stitches that are slipped often look distorted, but a good blocking will smooth out its appearance. The same is true for a garter stitch base, but the stockinette base shows the distortion more. Like regular slip stitches, all stitches are slipped purlwise and the working yarn is held toward the wrong side of the work.

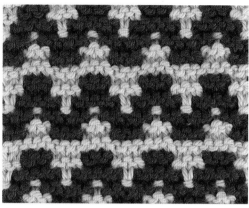

▲ Garter Stitch Base

▲ Stockinette Stitch Base

Charting Mosaics

There are two ways mosaics are charted. The first is used by Barbara G. Walker. In her books one row of the chart equals two knit rows. Second is when all rows are shown in the chart, as would be typical of most, if not all other types of knitting charts. I prefer Barbara G. Walker's method because the chart more closely resembles the finished work and with a regular chart it is redundant to show identical rows.

Since I am using Barbara G. Walker's charting method, looking at the chart, you will see that all rows are numbered on both sides and that one row of the chart represents two rows of knitting. Like all charts, you start at the bottom right corner and read the first row to the left. When coming back on the return row you do not even need to refer to the chart. Knit (for a garter base) the stitches you have knit and slip the stitches you have just slipped, meaning the same stitches are being worked and slipped as in the first row. If you want your design to have a stockinette base, you would purl the stitches on the return row and slip the stitches you have just slipped. Now you are back to the right side ready to start the third row color changes. You will drop the first color and pick up your second color and work two rows, continuing to alternate. To make a neat edge where the colors change, hold the yarn just worked to the right, pick up the new color from underneath, and work your next row.

On the chart, you will also notice the first and last vertical edges have alternating colors. Whatever color is on the edge, is the color you will be working across on that row. For example, if black is the edge color in the graph, then on this row you will be

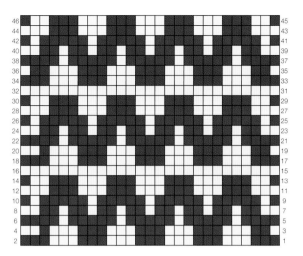

A. Barbara G. Walker's charting method. Note: the numbering of rows, one row of the chart equals two rows of knitting.

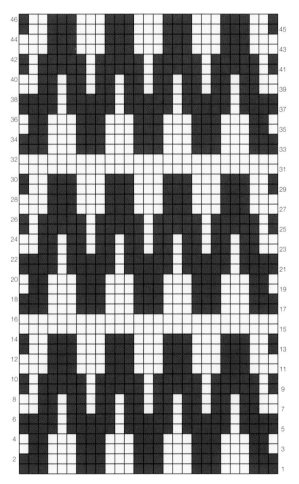

B. Regular Chart showing all rows. Note: the numbering of rows reflecting the right side and wrong side of knitting.

knitting the black stitches and slipping the white. Your cast on edge must be "white," the opposite color of the first edge stitch which is "black" or your first row will not have color changes. I will refer to all colors as black and white in the following instructions, but of course the sky's the limit to what colors you chose for your project.

Working through the chart

Referring to the mosaic chart A, it begins and ends with a black square in row 1. You will start by knitting the black square and continue reading the row to the left, knitting the black squares and slipping the white squares. Row 2 is the same: knit (or purl for stockinette stitched fabric) the black squares and slip the white squares. Right side facing, drop the black yarn towards the right and pick up the white yarn from underneath. Leave the black yarn hanging. For the next row the operation changes. Row 3 starts with a white square, so now you work the opposite; you will knit the white squares and slip the black squares. Row 4 is the same as row 3, knitting the white squares, slipping the black squares. Row 5 starts with a black square so you will reverse again and knit with the black squares and slip with the white

squares, continuing on in this way. If you come across a row that is all black or white, knit the whole row and returning row. There will be no slipped stitches on such rows.

Mosaic in the round

Cast on the amount of stitches needed for the multiple minus the edge stitches. Round one would be the same as in flat knitting; knit the black stitches and slip the white. Round two will continue the same as round one, purling the black stitches for a garter stitch fabric or knitting for a stockinette stitch fabric and slipping (with yarn behind) the white stitches. Round three will start with the white stitches being knit and the black stitches being slipped. Round four will be either a knit or purl row, depending on your choice of garter or stockinette stitch base as established and slipping the black stitches. Continue on with one color per two rows and in garter stitch or stockinette base.

When changing colors, pick up your new color to the left of the old and you will create a spiral. You can also pick up to the right, just be consistent with your choice and a spiral will form and keep the inside looking nice.

Slip Stitch & Mosaic Pattern Samples

The first three patterns in this section are a sampling of slip stitches. The last two patterns are mosaic patterns—one a garter stitch base and the other a stockinette stitch base.

RIC-RAC PATTERN

This simple slip stitch pattern is shown in two colors but would be very beautiful using three, four, or many multiples of colors. Every two rows the colors can be changed. This pattern can have the appearance of ribbing especially if a light hand is used in the blocking.

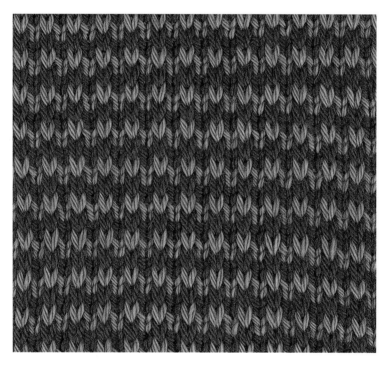

Odd Number of Stitches.
Two colors: A and B.

Row 1 (WS): With A, purl.

Row 2: With B, k1,*sl 1, k1; repeat from *.

Row 3: With B, purl.

Row 4: With A, k1, *sl 1, k1; repeat from*.

Row 5: With A, purl.

Repeat from row 2.

Ric-Rac Chart

Color A — K on RS, P on WS
X Slip St.

Color B — K on RS, P on WS
X Slip St.

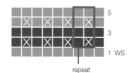

repeat

CHECK PATTERN

This cute check has the appearance of stranded knitting. The first row of this pattern has a straight row of color A, and looking at the swatch you might think this is a mistake, but A is the color that gets slipped and pulls over colors B and C.

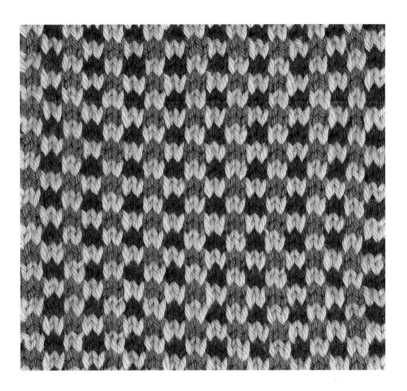

Multiple of 4 sts plus 2.
Three colors: A, B, and C.

Row 1(RS): With A, knit.

Row 2: With B, p1, *sl 2, p2; repeat from *, end p1.

Row 3: With B, k3, sl 2, *k2, sl 2 repeat from*, end k1.

Row 4: With A, purl.

Row 5: With C, k1, *sl 2, k2; repeat from *, end k1.

Row 6: With C, p3, sl 2, *p2, sl 2; repeat from *, end p1.

Repeat rows 1-6.

Check Pattern Chart

Color A   K on RS, P on WS
Color B   K on RS, P on WS
    X   Slip St.

Color C   K on RS, P on WS
    X   Slip St.

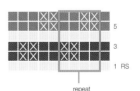

repeat

BLACK FOREST PATTERN

This pretty slip stitch has the added texture of a purl row. A very simple pattern to knit with a design that looks very complex.

Multiple of 4 sts plus 3.
Three colors: A, B, and C.

Row 1(RS): With A, knit.

Row 2: With A, purl.

Row 3: With B, k3, *sl 1, k3; repeat from *.

Row 4: With B, p3, *sl 1, p3: repeat from *.

Row 5: With C, k1, *sl 1, k3; repeat from *, end sl 1, k1.

Row 6: With C, k1, *sl 1, k3: repeat from *, end sl 1, k1.

Rows 7 and 8: With B, repeat rows 3 and 4.

Row 9: With A, repeat row 5.

Row 10: With A, p1, *sl 1, p3; repeat from *, end sl 1, p1.

Repeat rows 1-10.

Black Forest Chart

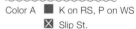

Color A	■ K on RS, P on WS
	☒ Slip St.
Color B	■ K on RS, P on WS
	☒ Slip St.
Color C	☐ K on RS, P on WS
	☒ Slip St.
	− P on RS, K on WS

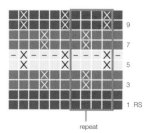

repeat

TREND MOSAIC

This handsome strong geometric pattern is made with a garter stitch base, so the wrong side rows are knit. This pattern could also be made with a stockinette base by changing the wrong side rows to purl. Follow instructions for mosaic knitting on pages 31 to 33.

Multiple of 18 sts plus 2 edge sts.
Two colors: A and B.
Follow chart.

Trend Mosaic Chart

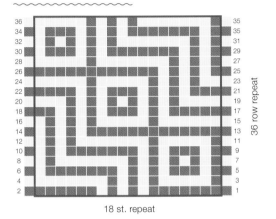

18 st. repeat

FLORENTINE MOSAIC

A beautiful zigzag pattern based on a background of stockinette gives this pattern a stranded knit appearance. By changing the wrong side rows from a purl to a knit, the base fabric becomes garter stitched and would be equally nice. Follow instructions for mosaic knitting on pages 31 to 33.

Multiple of 21 sts plus 2 edge sts.
Two colors: A and B.
Follow chart.

Florentine Mosaic Chart

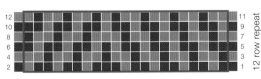

21 st. repeat

Slip Stitch Purse

Fast and simple, this purse is made with three colors using two different slip stitch motifs. A picot edge and I-cord strap finish it off in a cinch. To construct this purse, knit one side then pick up stitches from the bottom and work the second side. If you use a traditional cable cast on, there will be a slight ridge defining the bottom of the finished purse. Another choice is to use a provisional cast on (page 140) which provides live stitches to pick up, resulting in a smooth transition from one side to the other. If you use the provisional cast on, when you pick up your live stitches to work the second side of the purse, you will be one stitch short, so on that first row of the second side you will need to increase one stitch.

MATERIALS

1 each Lamb's Pride Worsted 85% Wool 15% Mohair; 4 oz (113 g), 190 yd (173 m) M-05 Onyx (A), M-04 Charcoal Heather (B), M-03 Grey Heather(C)

Size 6 (4.0 mm) needles straights and double points or size to obtain gauge

Size 5 (3.75 mm) needles or size to obtain gauge

Size 4 (3.50 mm) needles or size to obtain gauge

Gauge

22 sts and 37 rows = 4" (10 cm) over bottom half of purse Slip Stitch pattern with size 6 (4.00 mm) needle

Finished Measurements

8" (20.5 cm) high × 7" (18 cm) wide

Note: This pattern calls for three different needle sizes: one for the body of the purse, and two for the final five rows of the picot edge. The first three rows of the last five rows are worked with size 5 (3.75 mm) needles and the final two rows are worked with size 4 (3.50 mm) needles. Using the smaller size 4 (3.50 mm) needles will help make the inside hem circumference slightly smaller than the outside, giving you a well formed final picot hem.

Change to size 4 needles–

Change to size 5 needles–

Slip Stitch Purse

Note: on rows 53-54 and 69-70 the slip stitch is only 2 rows; all others are 4 rows

■ = A
■ = B
□ = C

M = Cable CO
B = BO
O = YO
\ = SSK
/ = K2tog
X = Slip st
— = K on RS, P on WS
⊠ = Slip st
■ = K on RS, P on WS
■ = K on WS
⊠ = Slip st
■ = K on RS, P on WS
◪ = SSK
◪ = K2tog

Purse

With size 6 (4.00 mm) needles and A,
Cable CO 37 sts.

Follow chart for pattern, color, and needle changes
to make the first side.

To make the second side, turn upside down, either
PU 37 sts if you used a traditional CO, or if using
the provisional CO, release the waste yarn and PU
the 36 live sts, remembering to increase one stitch
on the following row. Follow chart for second side.

Sew side seams. Fold top edge at the yo, k2tog row
to make a picot top, sew down on the inside.

Strap

With size 6 (4.00 mm) needles and A, CO
3 sts and make I-cord (page 141) for 52" (132 cm).
Weave straps through holes as pictured. Graft two
ends together.

Mosaic Coasters

Mosaic coasters are simple, fun, and easy to make. Firm and dense, they will protect table tops with style. Make all four different patterns or pick your favorite and make a set!

MATERIALS

1 each Lamb's Pride Worsted 85% Wool 15% Mohair; 4 oz (113 g), 190 yd (173 m) M-191 Kiwi (A), M-23 Fuchsia (B)

Size 6 (4.0 mm) needles or size to obtain gauge

Tapestry needle

Gauge

23 sts and 46 rows = 4½" (11.5 cm) in Mosaic Stitch on size 6 (4.00 mm) needles

Finished Measurements

4½" (11.5 cm) × 4½" (11.5 cm)

Instructions

With A, Cable CO 23 sts. Follow chart for pattern and color changes. With A, BO.

Note: Every row of chart represents 2 rows. Refer to pages 31 to 33 for instructions on how to knit garter stitch mosaic.

Mosaic Coasters Chart

■ = A   ■ = B

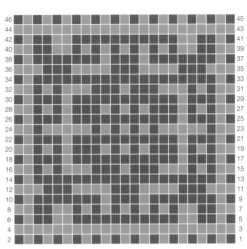

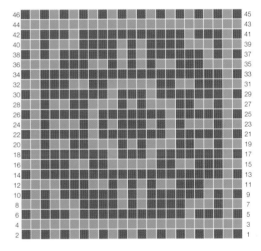

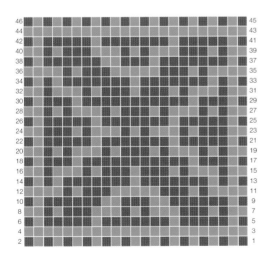

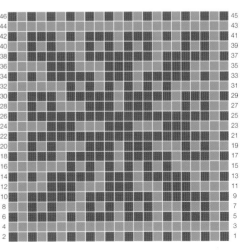

Mosaic Wristlets

Warm and soft, this wristlet is sure to be a hit. Knit flat and sewn for easy construction. Finish the edges with a crocheted picot, which adds femininity to the design.

MATERIALS

1 each Blue Sky Alpaca Sport Weight 100% baby alpaca; 1.7 oz (50 g), 110 yd (100 m) 541 Molasses (A), 545 Blue Spruce (B)

Size 4 (3.50 mm) needles or size to obtain gauge

Size D/3 (3.25 mm) crochet hook

Tapestry needle

Gauge

23 sts and 28 rows = 4" (10 cm) in Mosaic Stitch on size 4 (3.50 mm) needles

Finished Measurements

6½" (17 cm) high by 7¾" (19.5 cm) around wrist

Mosaic Wristlet Chart

Note: Every row of chart represents 2 rows. Refer to pages 31–32 for instructions on how to knit garter stitch mosaic.

■ = A
■ = B

With A, Cable CO 44 sts. Follow chart for pattern and color changes. BO in A on row 87. Block and sew seam to form a tube. With crochet hook and A, make a picot edge as follows: starting at top seam *chain 3, sl stitch twice*; repeat to end. Make matching picot on bottom edge. Make second wristlet.

STRANDING

Stranding is a technique that involves knitting with two different colors
of yarn per row, which can produce everything from simple to very intricate
colored knitting. The patterns of stranded knitting can look very complicated
in its color changes, but usually only two colors per row are used,
making them look more challenging than they really are.

Techniques

Often people call this technique Fair Isle, but Fair Isle is a type of stranded work, named after the Fair Isle, part of the Shetland Islands.

▲ Front

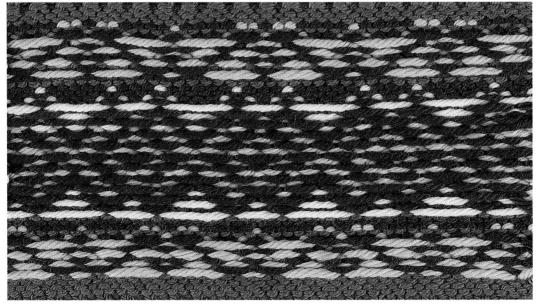

▲ Back

The word stranding describes what is happening during the color knitting process; the yarns "strand" behind as you work from one color to the next. These strands are also known as floats, and they're best seen from the back side of your knitting.

Stranded knitting can be found all over the world, but it is best known in countries that are colder, because when stranding you produce a double layered fabric that is thick and warm. Typically stranded knitting is done in stockinette stitch, but one exception is Bohus knitting which beautifully incorporates purl texture stitches.

When stranding there are many ways of holding the two different colored yarns; both colors in your left hand, both in your right, or one color in each hand. This is mostly preference, but I think it is to your advantage to use both hands. If you learn to knit using both hands you have the advantage of being able to easily purl with either hand. When you hold both yarns in one hand, the purl maneuver becomes a little trickier and most knitters do not like doing it. If you are always working a knit stitch (no purls) then you need to knit in the round.

The advantages for knitting in the round (always working a knit stitch) include always working on the right side of your work. This makes it easy to see the pattern or motif, and it eliminates seams. Knitting in the round produces a tube, so if you want to make a garment such as a cardigan, then a steek must be used. A steek is used wherever an opening needs to be made, at the center front, armholes and neck. They are extra stitches added to your knitting and are later cut open and finished off. There are different ways to finish off a steek depending on the type of yarn used. The disadvantage of a steek is the fear it raises in some knitters to cut their garments and the extra bulk it can produce. There is also some waste of your yarn in using a steek.

The advantage for knitting flat (working both a knit and a purl stitch) is it eliminates steeks, which therefore eliminates the bulk, and no wasting of yarn. The elimination of bulk is more important in a garment that is more close fitting and in the armhole if it is close set in. The disadvantage is not seeing the front of your work and for some having to purl. Knitting with both hands makes purling easy with practice. One big advantage of being able to purl is to easily make decorative two-color ribs and decorative textured edgings or to knit Bohus garments. Knitting flat does not mean you have to knit the front and back separately making a seam, garments are usually knit in one piece, so side seams are eliminated.

LEARNING TO KNIT WITH BOTH HANDS

When learning to knit, most beginners have difficulty holding on to the yarn and getting an even tension. It takes some time before it feels comfortable and natural. So learning to knit with your opposite hand will take practice to become comfortable and achieve an even tension. Remember there are many different ways to hold on to the yarn. Observe other knitters and see the variety of methods.

Knit a flat, one color stockinette swatch with your opposite hand to get a feel and some practice before making a practice swatch of two handed stranded knitting.

Holding Yarn in Right Hand (English or Throwing)

Wrap the yarn around your right hand middle finger for tension, but experiment and see what feels best for you. Your yarn must be able to freely pass through or your stitches will become too tight, and the opposite is true if the yarn is carried too loosely, your stitches will not be neat and tidy. If the yarn is fine, wrap the yarn twice around your finger. For a thicker yarn, place over your middle finger instead of wrapping.

Knit Stitch (white yarn)

1. With yarn in back, insert your needle from front to back into the first stitch on left-hand needle.

2. Throw your yarn from behind up and over the needle, pull through the loop forming a new stitch.

3. Slip the original stitch off of the left-hand needle.

Note: The brown yarn is not visible, but is held in the left hand.

Purl Stitch (white yarn)

1. With yarn in front, insert your needle from right to left in the front of the first stitch on left-hand needle.

2. Throw your yarn down over the needle, pull through forming a new stitch.

3. Slip the original stitch off of the left-hand needle.

Note: The brown yarn is held in the left hand, but is not being used.

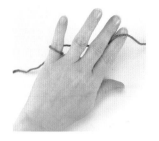

Holding Yarn in Left Hand, (Continental or Picking)

Wrap your yarn around your left hand pinkie finger, underneath your ring and middle finger and over your pointer finger for tension. Experiment for what feels best for you.

Knit Stitch (brown yarn)

1. With yarn in back, insert your needle from front to back into the first stitch on right-hand needle.

2. Wrap yarn up and over needle, pull through loop forming a new stitch.

3. Slip the original stitch off of the left-hand needle.

Note: White yarn is in the right hand, but not being used.

Purl Stitch (brown yarn)

1. With yarn in front, insert your needle from right to left in the front of the first stitch on left-hand needle.

2. Wrap yarn down over the needle, pull through forming a new stitch.

3. Slip the original stitch off of the needle.

Note: White yarn is in the right hand, but not being used.

Yarn in Both Hands

After experimenting with your opposite hand and getting a feel for the motion, it's time to try both hands. Do not pull hard on the yarn as you strand them across as this will produce puckering; just let the yarn gently carry across. Spreading the stitches on the right hand needle as you knit will help to keep your tension looser. However, do not be so loose that large stitches are produced.

Get in the habit of using one hand for the background and one hand for the motif. There are a few reasons for sticking with the same hand throughout a project. First, whenever you pick up your project you will not have to think about which hand you have been using and your motions for each hand will become automatic. Another advantage of keeping your yarn in the same hands is your yarns will not get twisted and tangled. In addition, your tension could be slightly different from one hand to the other. If this is the case you would want your tighter tension to be the background and your looser tension to be your motif. This way the motif would stand out more, versus being pulled back into the fabric. I have also heard to use your stronger hand (the one you always knit with when not doing stranded work) on the color that is used the most in the garment or project, which would typically be the background. The method I prefer is the Shetland way, which is to use the left hand for the motif and the right hand for the background. If you watch the path of the two yarns looking over the back of your work, you will see one color travels above which is the right hand and the other color travels below

which is the left hand. The Shetland rule is to use the color that travels under for the motif because it stands out most.

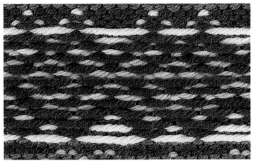

▲ Look closely at the back side of your knitting. The dark yarn is going over, and the white one is going under.

What is most important is to be consistent and carry your yarn in a way that is comfortable and that is as even a tension as you can produce. Every knitter's hand is different, and what works for one person might not work for another. As with all new skills, it could take some time and practice to learn the technique, but the end product is worth the effort. Within a project, always use the same hand positions. If you switch back and forth it will show because of your slight tension differences and because of the path the yarn travels, one above, one below, as stated before.

Tip: If your tension is too tight and the knitting is bubbling, one way to help is to work on circular needles and turn your knitting inside out. The outward curve will give that extra bit of yarn spread and could help with a too tight of tension.

GAUGE AND NEEDLE CONSIDERATIONS

Experiment with different needles. If your needle is very slippery, your stitches can fall off a bit too easily, especially if you like to work at the very tips of your needles. If it's too sticky, it's hard to slide your work across your needles. On circular needles it is particularly important to have a smooth join from the cord to the needle because you do not want to stop frequently and push your work over the join.

Your gauge can change from one type of needle to the next, so make sure when you make a gauge swatch you use the same type of needle for your project. Your gauge from stranded flat knitting to circular knitting is often different too. Often the gauge on circular knitting is looser.

Watch your gauge if you are knitting a garment or project that has areas of stockinette stitch. Stranding pulls the stitches together, so on the same size needles stranding will have a tighter gauge than stockinette. If there are only a few rows of stockinette, there is no need to change needle sizes but if there are larger areas it is best to change needles or to decrease some stitches. If you are working garter stitch to stranding, there is an even bigger gauge change, with garter stitch being quite loose in comparison.

Buy an extra ball of yarn in each color to make your gauge swatch. Then use your swatch to make a small project, like a small purse or coaster. This way you will also have some extra yarn on hand for any changes you might like to make, for example a little longer length to a garment. By keeping your swatch you will have a small record of what you made. A nice tip to help remember what size needles you have used on a swatch is to make knots on your tail to correspond with your needle. For example, for a size 4 (3.50 mm) needle make 4 knots in the tail.

YARN CHOICES

Any type of yarn will work for stranded knitting. For a traditional Fair Isle project, a Shetland style wool is best because of its properties. Shetland wool is soft, slightly twisted, and slightly hairy. Therefore, it is easy to steek, cut, and has the ability to gently felt. Wool yarn is often a good beginners' choice, as blocking will reduce tension or bubbling that can occur from pulling yarns too tightly across the back, a typical problem for a newer stranded knitter. Cottons and silk fibers work up beautifully in stranded knitting, but a consistent tension is necessary or else the colors will bubble and not look as nice. These fibers do not have the elasticity of wool, as a result, it will be difficult to fix or block out an uneven tension. A favorite fiber of mine is alpaca because it is soft and drapes well even as the fibers are stranded.

SPLICE

If you are working with a Shetland type wool it is easy to spit splice ends together. If your wool has a knot, then unknot it and unravel approximately 3" to 4" (8 to 10 cm) and pull half away. Do not cut because cutting will produce a blunt end, but pull it apart producing a ragged end. On the longer end if it was cut, pluck a bit at the end, taking away that bluntness too. Do the same to the other yarn.

Next, face the two ends together and wrap them around each other, trying to produce the same amount of thickness and same amount of spin.

Moisten your palm and briskly rub your palms together going over the whole area that was spliced. This will bond or felt the sections together.

READING CHARTS

Each square represents a color to be knit and the color changes that will occur. The bottom right corner is the starting point and reads across the row to the left. Typically the designs are small and repeat several times across a project. So your chart will have the edge set up area, a repeat area marked off, and maybe second edge area set up if needed. If you are working in the round, your chart is always read from right to left on each row, but if you are working flat, row 1 is read right to left and row 2 is read left to right.

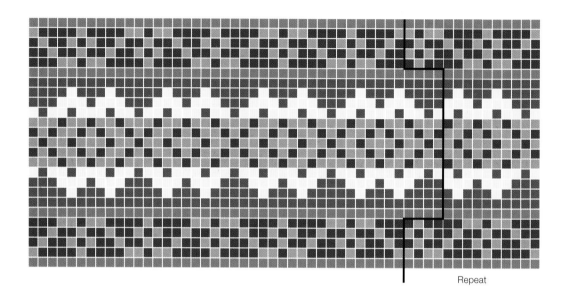

Repeat

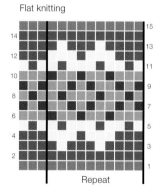

Flat knitting

Repeat

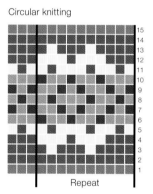

Circular knitting

Repeat

All charts reflect the garment or project about to be made and how the motif fits within the project. They are often marked for different sizes.

Tip: Some chart rows are easy to memorize, but others can be a bit more complex. On these more complicated rows, try to see the flow of what is happening. For example, many patterns have diamonds or diagonals. If you have a diamond shape, the shape will first be increasing and then decreasing. As you work along the row think: the diamond is growing larger, or the diamond is growing smaller. If you have a diagonal line think: it is moving one stitch to the left or one stitch to the right. A lot of patterns have symmetry and once you have worked a repeat or two you will see the rhythm and be able to work across your row without referring to the chart.

MAKING A GAUGE SWATCH

Remember when swatching for your project to use similar needles and the technique you'll use such as circular knit, or flat knit or a combination of both. Adjust your needle sizes if you are both circular and flat knitting in one project and your gauges are different. An example of such a project would be to make a pullover. You would circular knit to the underarms and then continue on your front and back separately by knitting them back and forth.

If you are circular knitting, you can knit a small flat swatch with this technique. Use a circular needle and always work on the front side by cutting your yarns at the edges. Cast on your stitches, knit to end. Cut yarn and slide work to other side of your needles, work across the front again. Continue until you have made a large enough swatch to get a gauge measurement. Because you are cutting yarns, you cannot unravel and reuse the yarns. Your edges will be loose or distorted, so measure your gauge in the middle of your swatch. If you do not want to cut your yarns, because you might need to reuse the yarn, just let a long float go behind the swatch. Make sure the float is long enough that you can lay the swatch flat for measuring.

WEAVING OR CATCHING LONG FLOATS

When stranding, sometimes a motif will have many stitches between color changes, and that would produce a long float. How often do want to catch a float? That all depends on your yarn and gauge. The most common number of stitches that you should not exceed is seven stitches or approximately 1" (2.5 cm) of stitches. This is really determined by your yarn choice, gauge, what the project is, and who it is being made for. For example, if you are making a garment for a child, you would not want long floats that little fingers could be caught in. If you are making a pillow, the floats would be enclosed so therefore not an issue, so leave the floats long.

When you weave a float, a small dimple could show on the right side, so take great care to not pull tight the float that is being woven. When you are weaving a float, try to weave it above the same color stitch as the row below.

Weaving long floats on the knit side

Weaving in left-hand yarn (white yarn)

1. Insert right-hand needle into stitch as if to knit.

2. Lift left-hand yarn over needle.

3. Wrap right-hand yarn to knit. Pull through, leaving left-hand yarn. Slide original stitch off needle.

Weaving in right-hand yarn (brown yarn)

1. Insert right-hand needle into stitch as if to knit.

2. Wrap right-hand yarn as if to knit.

3. Wrap left-hand yarn as if to knit.

4. Unwrap right-hand yarn.

5. Pull left-hand yarn through; stitch is made. Slide original stitch off needle.

1+2

3

4

5

Weaving long floats on the purl side

Weaving in left-hand yarn (brown yarn)

1. Insert right needle into stitch as if to purl.

2. Lay left-hand yarn over needle.

3. Wrap right-hand yarn over needle to purl. Pull through, leaving left-hand yarn. Slide original stitch off needle.

Weaving right hand yarn (white yarn)

1. Insert right needle into stitch as if to purl.

2. Wrap right-hand yarn under needle.

3. Wrap left-hand yarn over needle.

4. Unwrap right-hand yarn.

5. Pull left-hand yarn through; stitch is made. Slide original stitch off needle.

EDGE STITCHES WHEN WORKING FLAT

Both colors of yarn need to be attached at the edge, otherwise you will get a small hole. If one of your colors (A) is 4 stitches from the end and it does not get caught at the edge, you turn your work and start stranding and now the next time you use A and it is 5 stitches in. You will have just formed a small spread/almost a hole at that 4 stitch mark, because the yarn did not make it to the edge. The yarn pulled back on itself.

Three ways to catch at the edge

1. Work a float catch at the edge, as described on the previous page.

2. Trap unused color at the edge.

3. If the row you've just completed ends with color A, it is now attached at edge, the next row starts with color B, now it is caught at the edge. Both colors are attached to the edge.

FIXING JOGS WHEN WORKING IN THE ROUND

Just like in the stripes chapter when you work in the round while stranding, you form jogs. When designing, I try to put the jog in places to make it disappear as much as possible. On the Stranded Purse (page 77), I put the color changes on the edge where the green carries up the entire side. On the X O swatch (pages 72 to 73), the dark vertical stripe in the middle of the X would make a good spot to put the jog, the jog totally disappears or close to it. Sometimes you cannot find a good place to hide a jog, so then I use techniques like in the stripes chapter. On the stranded hat there is no place to hide the jog, so I did Jog Fix #2 (page 13): sliding the marker over one stitch with each row.

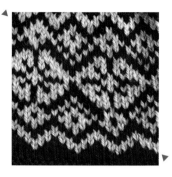

▲ Sliding one stitch over produces an almost invisible jog, only a very slight rise in the stitches can be seen, running from lower right to upper left.

Start of row ▲

◄ This chart shows the Stranded Hat chart doubled up as if it were being used for a pullover. The jog fix occurs exactly as on the hat, but on row 27 the yarns are cut and the jog fix is started over again. The red line shows the path of the shifting row start.

► Reusing the hat chart again, but this time with lots of color! Notice how easy it is to make many small jogs, all at the color change rows (indicated by the red line).

Start of row ▲

I also like to use Jog Fix #4 (page 14 and 15) on my stranded knitting. If you redesign the hat chart into an all-over pattern for a pullover, the design would repeat from the bottom to the top, and if you keep moving the first stitch one over, pretty soon you would be working across the front and heading towards the back of the pullover. A way to solve this would be with each round of a new motif, or colorway, move the first stitch back to the beginning spot. The yarns need to be cut with this method, which would happen anyway if you make a lot of color changes. Another option on a garment is to leave the jog and place it at the side seam. If you are using a fine yarn the jog may hardly be noticeable.

WORKING WITH MORE THAN TWO COLORS IN A ROW OR ROUND

Most stranded knit projects are knit with only two colors per row, but sometimes a design will call for more. You would need to carry two motif colors in the left hand and the background color in the right hand if you use my technique and hold yarns as the Shetland knitters do. You can also hold one of the motif colors and when you come to a color change drop it and pick up the next color. If the third color is just used here and there, then duplicate stitch would be the answer. Duplicate stitch is described on pages 116 and 117.

STEEKS

Steeks are the extra stitches used to make an opening in your knitting when knitting in the round, for example: the center front of a cardigan, the armholes or neck. These extra stitches are not part of the finished measured part of the sweater, but they make it possible to cut your knitted piece to make an opening. If you knit flat you will not need to make a steek.

There is a wide variety in the number of stitches used in a steek. Alice Starmore uses 10 stitches with the first and last as your edge stitches and the middle eight stitches being knit in a speckled pattern. Philosopher's Wool, *Fair Isle Sweaters Simplified,* uses one purl stitch. Ann Feitelson calls a steek a bridge pattern and uses twelve stitches that are knit in vertical striped lines. There are a variety of ways to make a steek and no one way is correct. It's a matter of personal preference and what your project needs are. The more steek stitches, the bigger the facing and the more stitches to have at your disposal when working bands, if some stitches become distorted or unravel.

▲ Five steek stitches in the speckled pattern are shown in this sample.

Your fiber will determine what type of steek you'll use and what finishing techniques to use. A Shetland style wool (very loosely spun or twisted) is one of the best yarns to use for steeks because of its natural tendency to softly felt and hold its stitches in place. Other fibers work well, too, but you will need to machine sew the steek to hold the stitches in place; examples are alpaca, machine wash and merino wools, cotton, silks, acrylic, and highly twisted wools, because they are smooth and slippery.

Follow these basic guidelines when knitting steeks:
- Either stripe or speckle your steek because it makes it firmer and less likely to unravel.
- When changing colors, change in the middle of the steek, then you will not need to finish off any ends in the body of your work.
- If you are steeking a neck or arm opening, you can still do all your shaping just outside of the steek.

FINISHING A STEEK

If you are using a Shetland type of yarn, the easiest way to finish it is to do nothing. Shocking but true, as the little ends will hang on and softly felt. Sometimes knitters will unravel and knot the ends together. If you wish, when planning your steek, do not add the steek stitches, just wrap your yarn around your needle 6 to 8 times. This will make long threads of yarn between your knitting. This will cause a bit of distortion at your edges, but they can be snugged back up when your knitting is finished. When finished knitting, cut down the middle. You can also darn in all these ends, but it's easiest to let them hang and felt, remembering it has to be a Shetland (fuzzy and self-felting) type of yarn! Another option if you have knit a striped or speckled steek is to hand sew down the facing that a steek produces.

Machine sewing is a common way of finishing a steek. Mark the center of your steek with a contrasting yarn. On the wrong side of your knitting you will have the ends of your yarns from where you changed colors at the center of your steek. You want them to get caught when sewing, but they need to be basted down first. Place your ends horizontally across the steek and either hand-baste or use a low tack tape (like artist's tape or painter's tape) to hold in place. If you use tape, do not leave it on your knitting, put it on right before you plan to sew and then immediately remove. Once ends are secured with basting or tape turn right side out. Set your machine to a small stitch setting (18–22sts per inch) and stitch on each side of your center contrasting yarn. Go over a second time if you feel you have not securely caught every strand or if you're using a slippery fiber that needs a second going over. Remove your center contrasting yarn and your basting or tape. Cut down the center between your machine stitched lines.

▲ Mark the center of your steek with a contrast yarn

▲ The inside of your work showing yarn ends

▲ Tape basting your ends down

▲ Machine sew on both sides of center. (green contrasting yarn has been removed)

▲ Cut steek apart

SUBSTITUTING COLORS

Sometimes a garment has the most beautiful design, but not in your favorite colors. Here are some tips to help change colors.

- Start by exchanging the dark with dark. For example, the design calls for a dark plum motif with multiple shades of light blue to green for the background, but you would like your garment to be blue and multiple shades of pink. The darkest color in the original is dark plum, you would replace that with a dark navy blue. Let's say the background colors of the original are one light blue, one soft green, and one heathery blue green. Your choices for replacing these colors could be pink, red, and fuchsia or pink, orange, and watermelon. The trick is to use colors that provide enough contrast between the background and the motif. The background colors in this example have multiple colors, and you do not want to have a lot of contrast between the background colors; they should blend. This does not mean they have to be in the same color family, say all pink, but they need to have the same value of color.

- To help tell whether colors have a similar or contrasting value, stack your yarns on top of each other, walk at least 6 feet away, and squint your eyes. If you are looking for contrast when you squint your eyes, you should see a big difference. The opposite is true if you are looking for colors to blend; when you walk away and squint no one color should jump out from the others.

- Finally, swatch! Colors that look perfect on a skein and held together can be totally wrong when you start knitting. Work out a swatch or two and come up with the perfect color combination.

Chart A

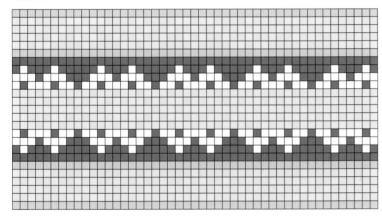

◀ These two charts show a perfect example of colors that work and colors that do not work. Only one color was changed. The gold color from chart A was changed to blue in chart B. The gold did not give enough contrast and the X and O was lost. In fact, the design on chart A appears to be three bands of color with a small amount of stranded work. The blue in Chart B gives a nice contrast and all motifs can be seen clearly.

Chart B

Stranded Pattern Samples

STRANDED PEERIES

Peerie patterns are small repeat patterns, two to seven rows high, used to separate larger motifs like the X and O (page 72). In this case, two are put together forming an all-over pattern.

Multiple of 14 sts plus 9 to center design.
Three colors: A, B, and C.

Follow chart for color changes.

Stranded Peeries Chart

☐ = A
■ = B
▩ = C

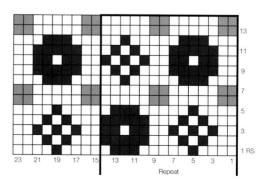

STRANDED DOT

A beautiful, all-over design of dots makes for an exciting pattern. With this array of color, you will have lots of ends. If you made a garment out of Shetland style wool, you could cut the ends and leave them. Another good option is to get two self-striping yarns, one light and one dark.

Multiple of 4 sts plus 2 to center design.
Eight colors: A, B, C, D, E, F, G, and H.

Follow chart for color changes.

Stranded Dot Chart

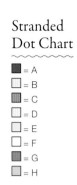

■ = A
□ = B
▨ = C
□ = D
□ = E
□ = F
▨ = G
▨ = H

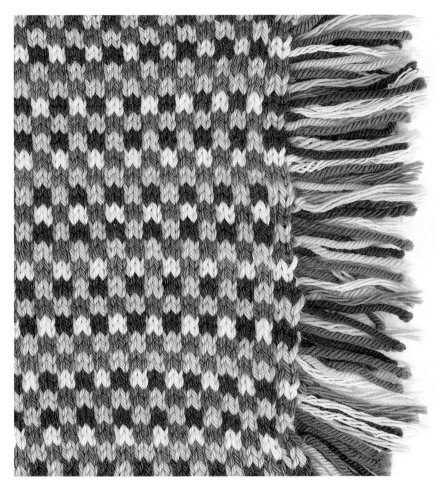

▲ The ends are shown, not to discourage you from making this design, but to make good yarn choices, like Shetland yarns or a self-striping yarn!

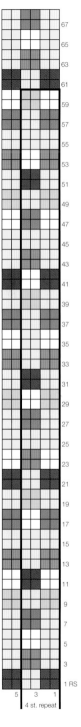

STRANDED ANATOLIAN

This design is Turkish and also goes by the name of Rose. The lovely scrolling shape works vertically and would typically be a design on a sock.

Multiple of 34 sts plus 3.
Three colors: A, B, and C.

Follow chart for color changes.

Stranded Anatolian Chart

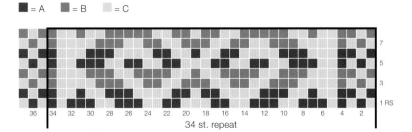

34 st. repeat

STRANDED STAR

Scandinavian stars grace the fronts of many exquisite sweaters. This pattern also has a simple but larger border surrounding the star.

Multiple of chart A (Border): 4 sts plus 1 to center design.
Multiple of chart B (Star): 20 sts plus 1 to center design.
Three colors: A, B, and C.

To make 3 star repeat (as shown) CO 59 sts.
Begin with chart A, then work chart B, finish with chart A.

Stranded Star Chart

☐ = A
▨ = B
■ = C

Chart A

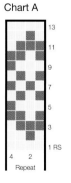

Chart B

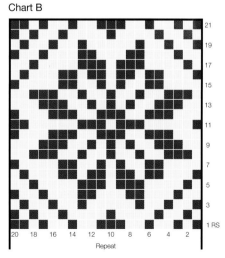

STRANDED X AND O

Common to Fair Isle knitting are many X and O patterns. There are so many beautiful O's it was hard to pick just one, so four have been included. A peerie of ric-rac with dots separates the bands in a subtle way.

Multiple of each square is 32 sts plus 1 to center the design
Six colors: A, B, C, D, E, and F.

Follow chart for color changes.

Stranded X and O

= A
= B
= C
= D
= E
= F

Stranded Projects

$\mathsf{Stranded\ Hat}$

Simple traditionally styled motif with a contrast edge makes a good choice for a first time circular stranded project. The motif is uncomplicated, making it easy to remember as you knit across the rows. To further aid, an explanation of the best way to hide a jog is included, so you can work through this project with ease.

MATERIALS

1 Each Louet Gems #2 Fine/Sport Weight Wool 100% Merino Wool; 3.5oz (100 g), 225 yd (205 m) 36 Linen Grey (A), 22 Black (B)

Size 2 (2.75 mm) 16" (40 cm) circular needle or size to obtain gauge

Size 3 (3.25 mm) 16" (40 cm) circular and double pointed needles or size to obtain gauge

Size 4 (3.50 mm) 16" (40 cm) circular needles or size to obtain gauge

Markers

Tapestry Needle

Gauge

25 sts & 32 rounds = 4" (10 cm) in Stranded knitting with size 4 (3.5 mm) needles

Finished Measurements

21½" (54 cm) around the brim × 7¼" (18 cm) high

Stranded Hat Chart

= A
= B

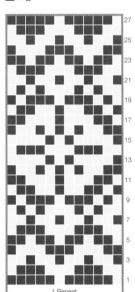

1 Repeat

Instructions

With size 4 (3.5 mm) circular needle and A, Cable CO 120 sts.

Change to size 2 (2.75 mm) circular needles. Join, being careful not to twist.

With B, work 3 garter st ridges as follows: (knit one round, purl one round) 3 times.

Next Round: Knit 1 row inc 12 sts by *k10, inc 1, repeat from* across, 132 sts.

Next Round: Knit.

Change to size 4 (3.5 mm) needles and work from chart.

Note: in order not to have a jog, slip the first stitch and move the beginning of the round over by one stitch with each round. See reference and chart on page 62 of the stranded section for fixing the jog.

When chart is finished change to size 3 (3.25 mm) needles and St st one row.

Next row decrease 4 sts evenly.

Work straight until hat measures 4¾" (12 cm). If you wish the hat to be longer, then add a few rows at this point.

Cap decreases

Round 1: *K2tog, k6, repeat from *.
Rounds 2 & 3: Knit.
Round 4: *K2tog, k5, repeat from *.
Rounds 5 & 6: Knit.
Rounds 7: *K2tog, k4, repeat from *.
Rounds 8 & 9: Knit.
Round 10: *K2tog, k3, repeat from*.
Rounds 11 & 12: Knit.
Round 13: *K2tog, k2, repeat from*.
Rounds 14 & 15: Knit.
Round 16: *K2tog, k1, repeat from*.
Rounds 17 & 18: Knit.
Round 19: K2tog across.
Round 20: K2tog across, 8 sts remain.

Cut tail and use to thread through loops and close up the hole.

Stranded Floral Purse

This colorful purse will give you practice in both flat knitting and knitting in the round. The purse starts at the bottom edge of the flap, knitting back and forth. When the flap is completed, stitches are added on to form the circular body of the purse. The body of the purse is worked upside down. The bottom edge is finished off with a three-needle bind off.

MATERIALS

1 each Rauma Finullgarn 100% Wool; 1.75 oz (50 g), 180 yd (164 m) 456 Pink (A), 439 Red (B), 4886 Fuchsia (C), 455 Green (D)

Size 2 (3.00 mm) 16" (41 cm) circular needle or size to obtain gauge

Size 3 (3.25 mm) 16" (41 cm) circular needle or size to obtain gauge

Markers

Tapestry needle

Gauge

28 sts and 30 rows = 4" (10 cm) over Stranded knitting on size 3 (3.25 mm) needles

Finished Measurements

6" (15.5 cm) wide × 8¼" (21 cm) tall

Tip: On the flap of the purse, cut motif yarn as the color changes are made, and work ends in when finished. On the body of the purse carry the three colors up the edge.

Tip: Usually the motif yarn would be attached to the outside edge stitches as explained on page 61, but because the edges of the purse are exposed, join it to the background stitches right where the motif and background meet: st 3 and st 41 on chart A.

Purse Flap

With size 2 (3.00 mm) needles and D, Cable CO 43 sts. Follow chart for color and needle size changes. Tip: on rows 5 and 6 at the left hand side, use the tail to knit the edge stitches so you do not have to weave the green yarn across the row and back. On rows 38 and 39 add a small piece of green yarn to the edge just like on rows 5 and 6, although it will be on the opposite edge.

Remember to change to size 3 (3.25 mm) needles on row 7 and back to size 2 (3.00 mm) on row 38, due to gauge changes.

Stranded Floral Purse Chart A

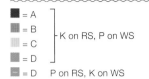

■ = A
▧ = B
▢ = C } K on RS, P on WS
▨ = D

▬ = D   P on RS, K on WS

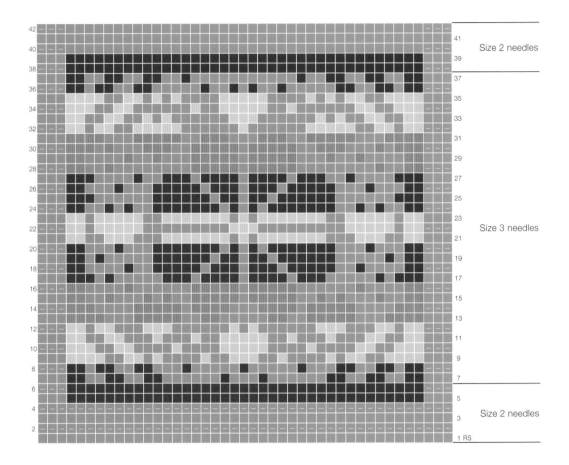

Size 2 needles

Size 3 needles

Size 2 needles

Body of Purse

After chart A is completed you will be on a right side row.

Cable cast on 43 sts and knit across both the new sts casted on and the front flap. Change to size 3 (3.25 mm) needles and join, work chart B two times (the front and back of purse) following color changes.

When chart B is completed turn purse inside out. Put front stitches on one needle and back stitches on another and 3-needle BO (page 141). Work in yarn ends and block.

Corded Strap

Instructions to make twisted cord are in Knitting Techniques on page 141.

Cord is made with 5¾ yd (5.3 m) of 1 strand each A, B, and C, and 3 strands of D.

Sew to outside edges leaving long tails.

Stranded Floral Purse Chart B

■ = A
■ = B
□ = C
■ = D

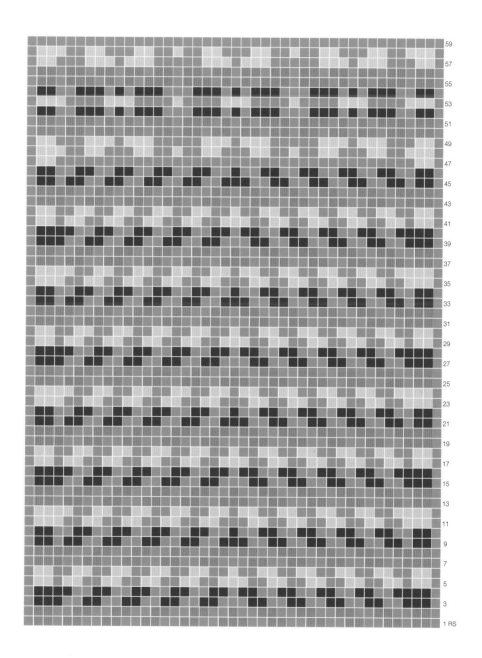

Stranded Collar Wrap

Colorful and warm, this pretty wrap will knit up quickly. Practice stranding using both knits and purls in this flat knit piece. Shaping is achieved by changing needle sizes as the work progresses. Feminine picots grace both edges along with a tie and crocheted buttons. Fun options—add pattern repeats and make a shrug (remember to buy more yarn), or flip the flowers upside down.

MATERIALS

1 each Frog Tree Alpaca Sport 100% Alpaca; 1.75 oz (50 g), 130 yd (118 m) 031 Medium Blue (A), 30 Light Blue (B), 57 Hot Pink (C), 26 Dark Rose (D), 25 Rose (E)

Size 2 (3.00 mm) 24" (61 cm) circular needle or size to obtain gauge

Size 3 (3.25 mm) 24" (61 cm) circular needle or size to obtain gauge

Size 4 (3.50 mm) 24" (61 cm) circular needle or size to obtain gauge

Size US F/5 (3.75 mm) crochet hook

Tapestry needle

Gauge

24 sts and 28 rows = 4" (10 cm) in Stranded knitting on size 4 (3.50 mm) needles

Finished Measurements

26" (99 cm) along bottom edge, 16½" (42 cm) along top edge, 7" (18 cm) high

Collar

With size 3 (3.25 mm) needles and A, Cable CO 129 sts.

Knit 1 row, p1 row.

Change to size 4 (3.5 mm) needles and work picot folding row: *k2tog, yo* repeat from *, end k1.

Purl 1 row.

Knit 1 row.

Purl 1 row.

Work 3 garter ridges:

With C, k 2 rows.

With D, k 2 rows.

With E, k 2 rows.

Next row: With A, knit.

Next row: Purl across dec 1 st. (128 sts)

Child's Cardigan

Cute and colorful, this child's cardigan is sure to please. This cardigan is knit in the round and steeked. It starts with a colorful textured rib, moving on to a stranded knit body section, followed by a textured and striped yoke, and ending with the textured ribbed collar. The steek is cut and front bands are then attached. This is a great project to work on for a first attempt at steeking.

MATERIALS

Shown: Louet Gems #3 Light/Light Worsted Weight 100% Merino Wool; 3.5 oz (100 g), 175 yd (160 m): 1 (1, 2, 2) skeins 42 Eggplant (A), 1 (1, 1, 2) skeins 48 Aqua (B), 67 Sea foam (C), 55 Willow (D), 39 Fern Green (E)

Size 3 (3.25 mm) 24" (61 cm) circular needles and double point needles or size to obtain gauge

Size 5 (3.75 mm) 24" (61 cm) circular needles and double pointed needles or size to obtain gauge 7 (8, 9, 11) ⅜" (1 cm) buttons

Locking stitch markers

Gauge

22 sts and 20 rounds = 4" (10 cm) in Stranded knitting on size 5 (3.75 mm) needles

20 sts and 28 rounds = 4" (10 cm) in Yoke pattern on size 5 (3.75 cm) needles

20 sts = 4" (10 cm) in Rib pattern on size 3 (3.25 mm) needles

Size

1 year, 2 years, 3-4 years, 5-6 years (shown in size 2 years)

Finished Measurements

Chest size: 23¾" (25", 26½", 28") 60.5 cm (63.5 cm, 67.5 cm, 71 cm)
Length measured from hem to top of collar: 10½" (12", 13¾", 14¾") 27 cm (31.5 cm, 35 cm, 37.5 cm)

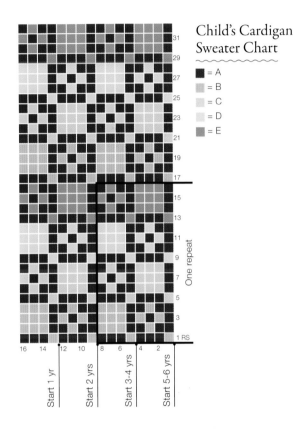

Child's Cardigan Sweater Chart

■ = A
▨ = B
▦ = C
□ = D
▨ = E

16 14 12 10 8 6 4 2

Start 1 yr
Start 2 yrs
Start 3-4 yrs
Start 5-6 yrs

One repeat

Rib Pattern

Round 1:*With A (eggplant) k1, with B (aqua) k1; repeat from *, end with A (eggplant) k1.

Round 2: *With A (eggplant) k1, with B (aqua) p1; repeat from *, end with A (eggplant) k1.

Round 3: *With A (eggplant) k1, with C (sea foam) k1; repeat from *, end with A (eggplant) k1.

Round 4: *With A (eggplant) k1, with C (sea foam) p1; repeat from *, end with A (eggplant) k1.

Round 5: With D (willow) knit.

Round 6: With D (willow) purl.

Sleeve Bands

With size 3 (3.25 mm) dpn and E (fern green), Cable CO 38 (42, 42, 46) sts. Work circularly and PM at beg of round, work rounds 1-4 of Rib Pattern. Slip 3 sts just worked back to LH needle. With D (willow) BO 6 sts. Knit to end. Place these 32 (36, 36, 40) sts on to a holder until ready to join to body. Make a second band.

Body

With size 3 (3.25 mm) circular needles and E (fern green), Cable CO 130 (138, 146, 154) sts. Place markers 2 sts in and before the final 3 sts. These 5 sts are your steek. While knitting over your steek, speckle the sts, refer to the technique on page 64. Steek sts will not be referred to with the rest of the instructions.

Join, being careful not to twist, and work rounds 1-6 of Rib Pattern.
Change to size 5 (3.75 mm) needles. Follow chart for pattern and color changes. End completing row 29 (33, 41, 49).

Next Round is both a dec round (k2tog), and binding off the underarm sts.
Work as follows: knit across with D (willow), dec 1 (1, 0, 1) st over RF 28 (30, 32, 34) sts, BO 6 sts,evenly dec 2 (4, 2, 2,) sts over back 57 (61, 65, 69) sts, BO 6 sts, dec 1 (1, 0, 1) over LF 28 (30, 32, 34) sts (not including steek sts).

Join sleeve bands to body
With D (willow), p across RF 27 (29, 32, 33) sts, PM, 1st sleeve band 32 (36, 36, 40) sts, PM, back 55 (57, 63, 67) sts, second sleeve band 32 (36, 36, 40)sts, PM, and LF 27 (29, 32, 33) sts. Total of 173 (187, 199, 213) sts (not including steek sts).

Yoke

To shape yoke refer to Yoke Stripe Pattern and individual sizes:

Size 1 year: Work Yoke Stripe Pattern repeat 3 times, adjusting pattern repeat by eliminating rounds 1 & 4, at same time do not dec on row 3 of 1st repeat only.

Size 2 years: Work Yoke Stripe Pattern repeat 3 times, and at same time do not dec on rounds 5 for all repeats.

Size 3-4 years: Work Yoke Stripe Pattern repeat 3 times, adjusting pattern repeat by adding an A (eggplant) p round after round 2 (on all repeats), and at same time do not dec on round 5 on 1st and 2nd repeats.

Size 5-6 years: Work Yoke Stripe Pattern repeat 3 times, adjusting pattern repeat by adding an A (eggplant) p row after both rows 2 and 11, and at same time do not dec on row 1 of 1st repeat only.

Yoke Stripe Pattern
Decrease round: *work to 2 sts before 1st marker, ssk, sl m, k1, k2tog, knit to 3 sts before 2nd marker, ssk, k1, sl m, k2tog, repeat from * to end.

Repeat rounds 1-13, 3 times for yoke, noting decrease rounds.

Dec Round 1: With D (willow) k.

Round 2: With A (eggplant) k.

Dec Round 3: With E (fern green) k.

Round 4: With C (sea foam) k.

Dec Round 5: With C (sea foam) k.

Round 6: With C (sea foam) p.

Dec Round 7: With B (aqua) k.

Round 8: With B (aqua) p.

Dec Round 9: With B (aqua) k.

Round 10: With E (fern green) k.

Dec Round 11: With A (eggplant) k.

Round 12: With D (willow) k.

Round 13: With D (willow) p.

61 (67, 71, 77) sts remain after 3 repeats are finished, (not including steek stitches).

Neck Band

Change to size 3 (3.25 mm) double pointed needles.

Round 1: *With A (eggplant) k1, with C (sea foam) k1; repeat from *, end with A (eggplant) k1.

Round 2: *With A (eggplant) k1, with C (sea foam) p1; repeat from *, end with A (eggplant) k1.

Round 3: *With A (eggplant) k1, with B (aqua) k1; repeat from *, end with A (eggplant) k1.

Round 4: *With A (eggplant) k1, with B (aqua) p1; repeat from *, end with A (eggplant) k1.

Round 5: With E (fern green) knit.

Round 6: With E (fern green), BO in purl st.

Cut and finish steeks

Machine stitching is recommended.

Front Bands

Left Front
With size 3 (3.25 mm) needles and D (willow), PU 55 (63, 71, 85) sts.

Next Row(WS): knit.

Row 1(RS): *With A (eggplant) k1, with C (sea foam) k1; repeat from *, end with A (eggplant) k1.

Row 2(WS): *With A (eggplant) p1, with C (sea foam) k1; repeat from *, end with A (eggplant) p1.

Row 3: *With A (eggplant) k1, with B (aqua) k1; repeat from *, end withA (eggplant) k1.

Row 4: *With A (eggplant) p1, with B (aqua) k1; repeat from *, end with A (eggplant) p1.

Row 5: With E (fern green) knit.

Row 6: With E (fern green) BO in knit st.

Right Front
Make RF to match LF, making 7 (8, 9, 11) buttonholes as follows: on row 2 in pattern work 2 sts *p2tog, yo, work 6 sts in pattern; repeat from *, end working in pattern 3 sts. Note the p2tog is an A (eggplant) st oriented 1st, then the C (sea foam).

Finishing
Block cardigan and sew on buttons.

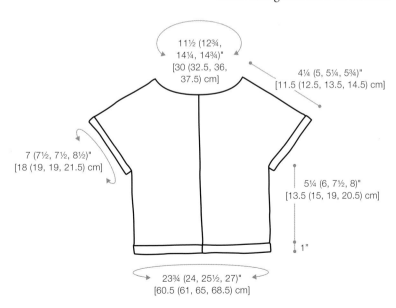

11½ (12¾, 14¼, 14¾)"
[30 (32.5, 36, 37.5) cm]

4¼ (5, 5¼, 5¾)"
[11.5 (12.5, 13.5, 14.5) cm]

7 (7½, 7½, 8½)"
[18 (19, 19, 21.5) cm]

5¼ (6, 7½, 8)"
[13.5 (15, 19, 20.5) cm]

1"

23¾ (24, 25½, 27)"
[60.5 (61, 65, 68.5) cm]

INTARSIA

Intarsia is a technique used to make motif or picture knits,

requiring separate balls of yarn to create

the different areas of color.

Techniques

Intarsia is completely different from stranded knitting. In stranded knitting both of your yarns are carried from edge to edge of your work; with intarsia the yarns go from color block to color block and interlock. On the wrong side of your knitting you will see it does not have the double thickness that stranding has.

Another difference between stranded and intarsia is the amount of colors used per row. In stranded knitting, typically two colors per row are used, but in intarsia there can be just a few colors to many colors per row. Generally intarsia is knit in stockinette stitch, but other stitches can be added too.

The main technique with intarsia is the twist or interlock of one color to the next. Twisting is one term often used for intarsia but a better term is interlock. In this chapter, twisted will refer to something tangled up! If you do not interlock your color changes, you will produce holes in your work.

Knitters seem to love or hate intarsia. In order to love intarsia you need to embrace the fact that

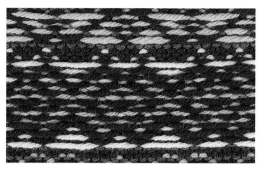

▲ Back of stranded knitting

there could be many yarns to deal with and ends to work in. There are ways to manage all this chaos, and at the end of all your hard work you will produce a beautiful piece of knitting.

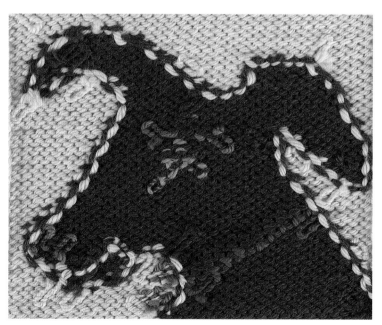

▲ Back of intarsia knitting

DIVIDING UP THE YARNS

The first consideration when starting an intarsia project is the dividing of your colors. Often knitters will put their yarns onto bobbins. There are various sized and styles of bobbins available. Practice with different ones and see what you like. You can also make a butterfly. A butterfly is made by wrapping the yarns around your fingers, essentially making a small center pull ball. If your yarns get tangled it is easier to pull your small ball apart and rewrap it after the yarns are free.

How to make a butterfly

1. Hold on to to your yarn end with your last three fingers closed over the yarn in the palm of your hand.

2. Wrap your yarn around your thumb and pointer finger making a figure 8. Cut yarn leaving a 8" (20 cm) tail.

3. Carefully slide off your fingers and wrap tail tightly around center of butterfly, sliding the end under last wrap.

4. The butterfly is a center pull mini-skein so pull from the end that was held under your last three fingers.

If you need only a small amount of yarn, two or three yards (meters), do nothing, just let it hang. If you need larger amounts, use the skein or use a center pull ball.

To calculate how much yarn you will need for an area, you can count up the squares on the chart and wrap your yarn around your needle the same amount of times. Remember to give yourself a little extra and for working in your ends. This is just a rough estimate but will get you close. When you make your gauge swatch, you can see how accurate this was and adjust for your project.

TWISTING YARNS

There are many ways of controlling your yarns from twisting and tangling. There are bowls and boxes to buy or you can put your yarns in baggies. The trick is to be able to pull your yarns out freely, yet not so much that you have a lot of excess yarn out to tangle. You might find it easiest to do nothing but put all the yarns to your left side. When you have finished working a right side row, turn your needles counter clockwise. You will see with that first knit row you have put a twist onto each yarn. Then when you finish your purl row, turn your needle clockwise and all your yarns will be untwisted.

Do not agonize if your yarns get twisted; continue working as long as you can pull the yarn through. If you get to the point when it's too tangled, then stop and untwist. This is the point where knitters get frustrated, but your yarn does not need to lie perfectly and it is okay for it to be a bit disorderly; you will still produce beautiful knitting. Another frustrating part can be when your knitting is finished and you have to work in all those ends. Put on a good movie or think of it as meditation!

INTERLOCKING

Whether you are on the knit side or purl side the technique is the same. **When you come to the point where you want to change colors, hold the color just used to your left and pick up the new color from the row below and place over the yarn just used.** Begin knitting or purling

▲ Vertical Interlock Knit

▲ Vertical Interlock Purl

depending on which side you are on. Leave the yarn not in use dangling until you are on your next row. Then pick it up and use it again. If you are done with a color, cut it off with a decent length tail to weave in, so there is one less yarn to tangle.

Intarsia designs are not only vertical, but can be organic and move in diagonals. The following pictures show the front and back of the stitches moving left and right. You will see this effect on Rosie Dog pattern and others.

▲ Left Diagonal Knit. Light is dropped to the left; dark is picked up from below and brought over light.

▲ Right Diagonal Knit. Dark is dropped to the left; light is picked up from below and brought over dark.

▲ Left Diagonal Purl. Light is dropped to the left; dark is picked up from below and brought over light.

▲ Right Diagonal Purl. Dark is dropped to the left; light is picked up from below and brought over dark.

You will find that the points where you add and drop colors look messy and you are forming holes. When you work your ends in, all these start and stop points will close and neaten up.

One very important point when interlocking colors is to not be tempted to strand behind a stitch or two because you are trying to cut corners and do not want to add on another new color. The stitches that are stranded will not be interlocked and will fold in and be distorted. Your finished product will not have a consistent appearance.

Sometimes when starting a new color you might miss an interlock. If this happens you can use a tapestry needle and manually interlock it. If you find when your work is done a stitch is slanting in an undesirable way, you can straighten the stitch out with a manual interlock. Use a separate yarn, work in your tail, interlock the stitch, and work in your tail. (Shown at right with orange yarn for clarity.

If your stitches are distorted, use your knitting needles to manually smooth them out. When locking a vertical line it is not unusual to have a tight stitch then a loose stitch, so again use your needle to manually adjust them. This is often easiest when done from the back by sliding a knitting needle behind the vertical loops.

MIXING INTARSIA WITH STRANDING

First, do not strand from one color block area to another—that will only distort your stitches. Use separate balls for that. But if you want to strand within a motif, this will work. **When interlocking, always make sure that both the stranded colors are being treated as one.** So when interlocking your single yarn it will go over both stranded stitches and the opposite is true when you are interlocking your double strands over the single yarn.

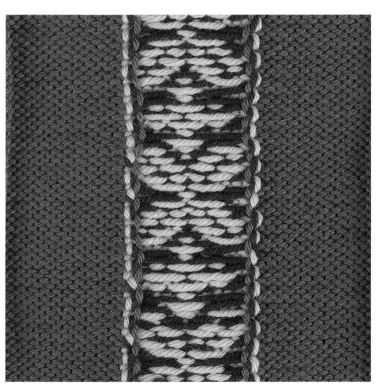

INTARSIA STRANDED MIX

This swatch shows a correct mixing of intarsia with stranding. Notice the stranding is contained within the cream color block. The intarsia interlock happens where the vertical sections meet.

Three colors: A, B, and C.

Intarsia Stranded Mix Chart

■ = A
■ = B
□ = C

Cable CO 12 sts with A, 13 sts with B, and 12 sts with A.

Using both the intarsia and stranding techniques, work back and forth in stockinette stitch following chart for color changes.

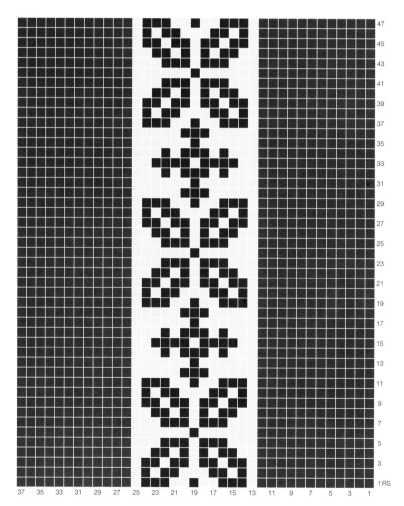

INTARSIA CAT

A cute kitty is the perfect way to practice your intarsia technique. Colors in ears, eyes, nose, and collar are duplicate stitched (page 116) after the cat's body and background are completed, making this an easy first intarsia. The whiskers are straight stitched on top as the finishing touch. This cat design and chart can be used as a variation to the Owl Hat. If using on the hat, stem stitch the whiskers for more stability.

Six colors: A, B, C, D, E, and F.

Intarsia Cat Chart

- ☐ = A   ▨ = B
- ■ = C   ▨ = D
- ▨ = E   ▨ = F
- ●━━━● Straight stitch with C

(Note: straight stitch can go between or into middle of stitches.)

Cable CO 4 sts with A, 23 sts with B, and 4 sts A.

Using the intarsia technique, work back and forth in stockinette stitch following chart for color changes.

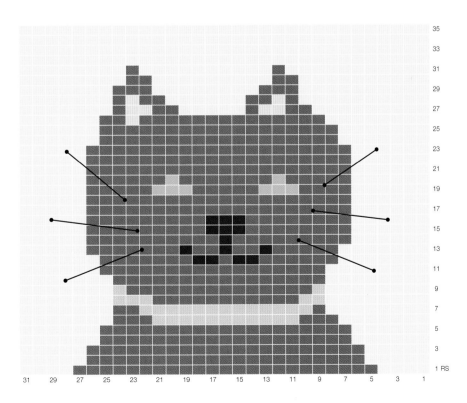

INTARSIA ROSIE DOG

Try out your intarsia skills on this playful pup. To make the intarsia easier, duplicate stitch the eyes, eye brows nose, mouth, and collar when the dog and background are completed. This dog design and chart can be used as a variation to the Owl Hat.

Five colors: A, B, C, D, and E.

Intarsia Rosie Dog Chart

- ■ = A
- □ = B
- ▨ = C
- ▨ = D
- ▨ = E

Cable CO 19 sts with A and 12 sts with B.

Using the intarsia technique, work back and forth in stockinette stitch following chart for color changes.

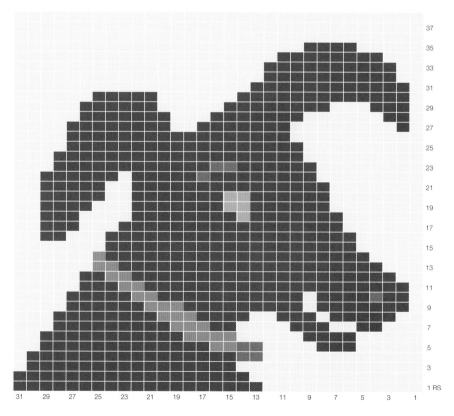

INTARSIA HEART

A three-colored heart design uses the intarsia technique and also incorporates purl stitch texture, in the form of seed stitch. Like the Intarsia Cat and Intarsia Rose Dog, this heart design and chart can be used as a variation to the Owl Hat.

Four colors: A, B, C, and D.

Intarsia Heart Chart

⬜ = A
⬛ = B, K on RS, P on WS
⬛ = B, K on WS
⬛ = C, K on RS, P on WS
⬛ = C, K on WS
⬛ = D, K on RS, P on WS
⬛ = D, K on WS

With A, Cable CO 31 sts.

Using the intarsia technique work back and forth following chart for color changes and texture stitches.

Intarsia Projects

Intarsia Pillow

This charming pillow is made as a complement to the Striped Pillow on page 23. The blocks of color are asymmetrical and alternate from front to back, so by flipping the pillow from front to back or top to bottom, you can change the look on a whim.

MATERIALS

1 each Blue Sky Alpaca Worsted Cotton 100% Cotton; 3.5 oz (100 g),150 yd (137 m): 618 Orchid (A) 640 Hyacinth (B), 633 Pickle (C), 632 Mediterranean (D), 624 Indigo (E)

16" × 16" (41 cm × 41 cm) Pillow form

Size 7 (4.5 mm) 24" (61 cm) circular needles

Bobbins (optional)

Tapestry needle

Gauge

16 sts and 22 rows = 4" (10 cm) in Stockinette Stitch on size 7 (4.5 mm) needles

Finished Measurements

16" × 16" (41 cm X 41 cm)

Instructions

With size 7 (4.5 mm) needles and A, CO 66 sts. Work from chart A changing colors as indicated. When chart A is completed do not BO, but begin chart B. BO when chart B is completed.

Block pillow.

Fold the fabric in half along the color change from chart A to chart B. Sew side seams. Insert pillow form. Sew bottom edge.

Intarsia Pillow Charts

█ = A
█ = B
█ = C
█ = D
█ = E

Chart A

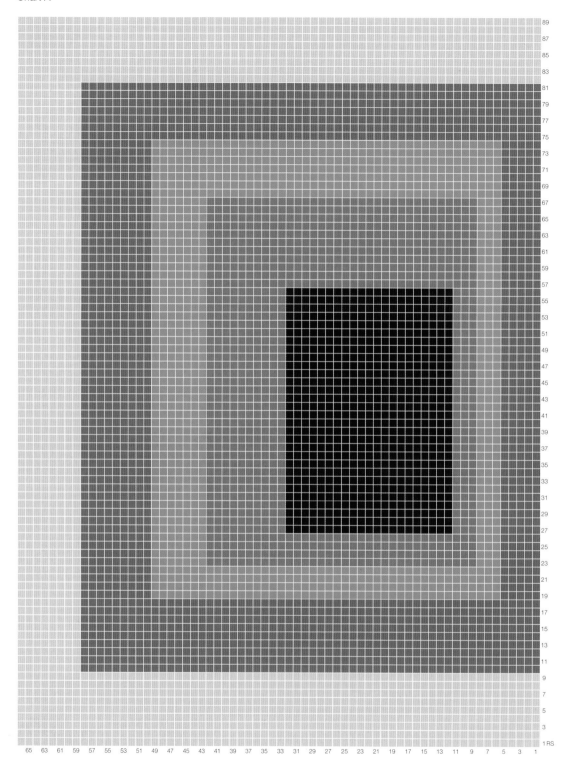

Chart B

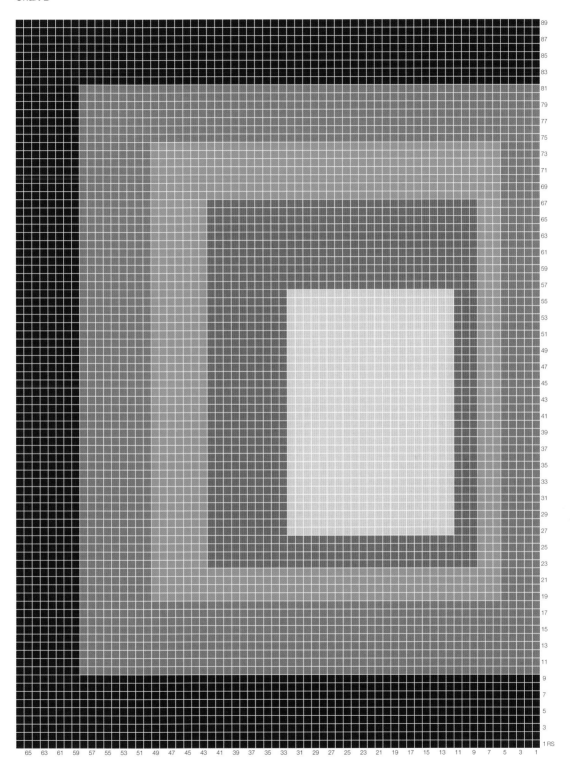

Intarsia Daisy Purse

A sweet daisy flower adorns this pretty purse. To add interest, a coiled I-cord makes for an attractive handle. The green stems and the flower centers can be knit in as you go or could be duplicate stitched on afterwards. Cording is worked into the straps for some extra stability.

MATERIALS

Shown: Lamb's Pride Worsted 85% Wool 15% Mohair; 4 oz (113 g), 190 yd (173 m): 1 skein each M115 Oatmeal (A), Autumn Harvest (B), M14 Sunburst Gold (C), M155 Lemon Drop (D), M191 Kiwi (E)

Size 6 (4.00 mm) needles straights and double points or size to obtain gauge

Bobbins (optional)

Tapestry needle

Cording to put inside straps

Bodkin

Gauge

22 sts and 32 rows = 4" (10 cm) in Stockinette Stitch on size 6 (4.00 mm) needles

Note: This gauge is on the tight side so the purse will be a bit firmer.

Finished Measurements

6" (15.5 cm) high × 12" (30.5 cm) wide at base, narrowing to 10" (25.5 cm) at top

Note: To construct this purse, knit one side, then pick up stitches from the bottom and work the second side. There are two different types of cast on. The first decision is which cast on you would like to use. If you use a traditional cable cast on, there will be a slight ridge on the bottom edge of the finished purse. This is not a big issue; feel free to use this cast on if you want. However, another choice is to use a provisional cast on. If you use a provisional cast on, you will have live stitches to pick up and you will not have a ridge. Directions for provisional cast on are on page 140. If you use the provisional cast on, when you pick up your live stitches to work the second side of the purse you will be one stitch short, so on that first row of the second side you will need to increase one stitch.

Intarsia Daisy Purse Chart

- = A
- ▥ = B
- ▦ = C
- = D
- ▨ = E
- ⟋ = k2tog
- ⟍ = ssk
- X = attachment point for coiled straps
- ⁻ = p on RS, k on WS

Instructions

With size 6 (4 mm) needles and A, CO 61 sts using either a traditional or provisional CO.

Follow chart for shaping and color changes.

To make the second side, turn upside down, either PU 61 sts if you used a traditional CO, or if using the provisional CO, release the waste yarn and PU the 60 live sts, remembering to increase one stitch on the following row. Follow chart for second side.

Block. Sew side seams. Sew bottom side seam gusset.

Straps

Make 2.

With size 6 (4 mm) dpn needles and A, CO 5 sts and make I-cord for 32" (81.5 cm). Directions for I-cord on page 141. Leave 12" (31 cm) tails for sewing straps to the body of the purse. With a bodkin, pull 2 or 3 pieces of cording into straps (number of pieces depends on the thickness of your cording). Make sure the cording is worked into the center and does not show on the right side.

Using picture and chart symbol X as a guide, coil and sew down straps to the front and back of purse.

If desired, visit a framing store or artist supply store and buy a piece of matching mat board and cut to fit the bottom of the purse for stability.

Intarsia Owl Hat

For a little challenge, try this small project that uses intarsia and stranded knitting techniques combined. At the same time this design is simple and cute! The intarsia samples of Intarsia Cat, Intarsia Rosie Dog, and Intarsia Heart can easily be substituted in the center of this hat, making this four hats in one.

MATERIALS

Shown: Frog Tree Alpaca Sport 100% Alpaca; 1.75 oz (50 g), 130 yd (118 m)

2 skeins in 37 Blue (A)

1 skein each 308 Dark Blue (B), 0012 Dark Brown (C), 000 Cream (D), 007 Brown (E), 009 Grey (F), 008 Warm Brown (G), scrap of 91 Gold (H)

Size 2 (3.00 mm) needles or size to obtain gauge

Size 3 (3.25 mm) needles (second set for 3-needle BO) or size to obtain gauge

Markers

Bobbins (optional)

Tapestry needle

Gauge

24 sts and 32 rows = 4" (10 cm) in Stockinette Stitch on size 3 (3.25 mm) needles

30 sts and 32 rows = 4" (10 cm) in Stranded knitting on size 3 (3.25 mm) needles

Finished Measurements

Approximately 20" (51 cm) at band, 22" (56 cm) above the band by 7" (18 cm) high

Garter Stitch Ribbing

Row 1(RS): *With A, k1, with B, k1, repeat from *.

Row 2: *With B, p1, with A, k1, repeat from *.

Repeat rows 1 and 2.

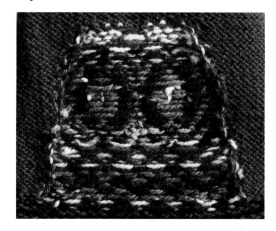

Notes: Hat is knit flat and uses both intarsia and stranded knitting techniques. Read about this technique on page 95.

All sample design charts (Intarsia Cat, Rosie Dog, and Heart) are 31 sts (instead of 37 like the owl chart). If you want to substitute one of these designs, follow the numbers placed in parentheses. If only one number is given in the direction, then it applies to both the owl chart and any of the sample design charts

A chart is used over the center front 37 (31) sts. Markers are placed on the hat to define these 37 (31) sts.

Pay close attention to the finishing. The hat top has a 3-needle BO in the side-to-side direction. The back center seam is sewn from the ribbing to the top. Next the two top corners are folded and stitched down at the top, at the center back seam.

Tip: Duplicate st the beak and eye centers.

Intarsia
Owl Hat Chart

■ = A
■ = C
□ = D
■ = E
■ = F
■ = G
□ = H
⧄ = k2tog
⧅ = ssk

Instructions

With size 2 (3.00 mm) needles and B, Cable CO 134 sts.

Work garter stitch rib for 1" (2.5 cm), ending on a WS row.

Looking at the RS of your hat, place markers on your needles counting from right to left: count 49 (52) sts, PM, count 37 (31) sts, PM, end with 48 (51)sts. 134 sts.

Change to size 3 (3.25 mm) needles and A.

Increase Row: Knit 49 (52) sts evenly inc 3 sts, sl m, begin owl chart (using stranding technique and remembering to interlock both stranding yarns from owl to the one yarn of background A, or sample design charts across center 37 (31) sts, sl m, knit 48 (51) sts evenly inc 4 sts (141 sts).

Continue in St st as established following owl chart (or sample design charts) over center 37 (31) sts. On final row of owl chart 6 sts are decreased. If using sample design chart when chart is completed on next row evenly decrease 6 sts. (135 sts)

When finished with chart continue knitting straight until hat measures 8½" (22 cm). Cut 12" (31 cm) tail.

Set up for 3-needle BO: On back count 34 sts, PM, on front count 67 sts, PM, 34 sts left on the other back half. With RS facing each other place front sts on one needle and two back halves on another.

Using new yarn (not 12" [31 cm] tail) and with the back of the hat facing you, 3-needle BO, top of the hat (page 141). There is one extra stitch on the back needle (side facing you); when you get to the center back opening, BO 2 center back sts together along with one stitch from the front needle, which closes the back seam. See the photo below. Continue binding off to the end. Leave 8" (21 cm) tail.

▲ Place needle into the first 2 sts on front needle and then through first st on back needle. Wrap yarn and pull through all sts.

Using 12" (31 cm) tail sew back seam.
Fold points to the top of center seam, use 8" (21 cm) tails to sew down.

DUPLICATE STITCH, EMBROIDERY & DECORATIVE EMBELLISHMENTS

A stunning and creative way to personalize your knitting
is to embellish or add color on the top surface. You can achieve this
by adding embroidery stitches, ribbon, or anything
decorative onto your knitting.

Techniques

DUPLICATE STITCH

Duplicate stitch is a common way to add more color and design to a knit project. It is often used in intarsia for small bits of color areas. Stranded knitters also use duplicate stitch as a way to bring in more colors than the usual two colors per row. Duplicate stitch is embroidery that exactly matches a knit stitch. Because of this, it will look as if you knit the color in while you were working the row.

▲ The dark blue outline of the butterfly is duplicate stitched.

Wherever you duplicate stitch, your fabric will be slightly denser and somewhat stiffer. Typically you would use the same weight of yarn, although you could use finer, but your base fabric will show through. Sometimes it is nice to use a yarn that is fuzzier, because the fuzz will help hide the base fabric.

Another tip for choosing yarns for duplicate stitch is to use a plied yarn, such as wool Persian needlepoint yarn. That way you can use one, two, or three plies or whatever amount you need to cover the base stitch. Also, Persian needlepoint yarn comes in a large variety of colors and you can buy it in small amounts. If your yarn is not covering your base stitch completely, try twisting in an extra ply to your duplicate stitch yarn.

You can use charts from cross stitch patterns and duplicate stitch the design onto your project. Remember that in knitting, your gauge is rarely square; usually charted it would look like a rectangle. So if you are using a cross stitch chart, know that your duplicate stitched design will be squashed, a little or a lot depending on your knitted gauge. Depending on the chart this may be fine, or make adjustments to your graph on knitting graph paper.

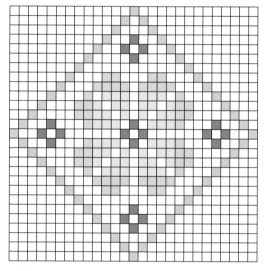

▲ Cross stitch chart

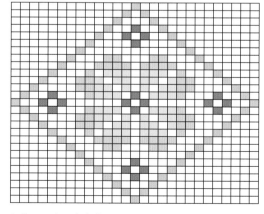

▲ Same chart in knit gauge

Start your duplicate stitching by reading the chart as you would to knit. Start at the right bottom corner of the design.

1. Thread your yarn onto a large eye tapestry needle.

2. From the wrong side bring your needle to the right side, through the stitch below where the first stitch is to be made.

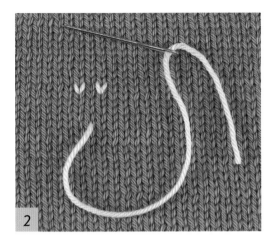

3. Pass the needle from right to left under the stitch above.

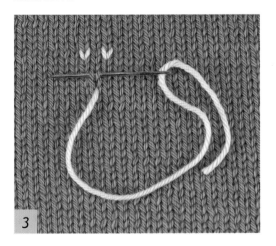

4. Dive the needle into the same hole where you first brought the yarn up.

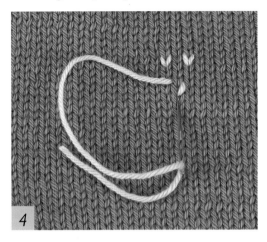

5. Bring your needle to the right side, into the center of the next stitch to be made. Work as in steps 3 and 4.

Continue in this manner for the number of stitches needed.

If your chart moves you to the next row above, you will work left to right. This is often easier if you turn your work upside down. Next row turn your work right side up again, continuing in this manner.

You will see as you make your duplicate stitches that you are exactly mimicking your base knitting. Also for the best results, dive your needle up and down for each step of the duplicate stitch. This way the new color will lay directly on top, giving good coverage of the base stitch.

EMBROIDERY

In this section, only the most basic of stitches are shown: French knots, detached chain stitch, stem stitch and straight stitch. These are the most common and will give many options for creating beautiful designs. Also, look through embroidery books and be inspired for new stitches and new designs. When embroidering on fabrics, often your work is put onto hoops or stabilized with special embroidery paper. Typically with knitting, these products are not needed, but it's always best to experiment and determine whether or not your knitting needs some stability and use the appropriate product from a craft store.

French Knot

A French knot is made by wrapping your yarn around your needle twice, but with some yarns that will make too large a knot, so then only wrap once. If you want a larger knot wrap three times.

1. From wrong side bring your needle to the right side.

2. Wrap the yarn around your needle two times.

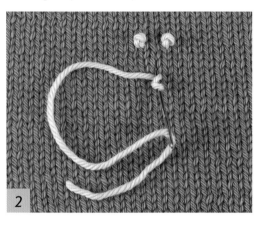

3. Keep a light tension on your yarn and dive your needle down, preferably in the next stitch. If you dive back into the same spot, the knot could sink to the back side of your knitting.

4. Pull your yarn to the wrong side, making your first knot.

Detached Chain Stitch (Lazy Daisy)

This easy stitch is often used in a circle to form a flower.

1. From wrong side bring your needle to the right side.

2. Dive your needle back into the same spot, keeping a loop of thread on the right side.

3. Bring your needle up from the wrong side, through the loop that is formed near the top.

4. Dive your needle over the top of the loop to the wrong side with a short stitch.

One chain is formed. Make as many as needed to form design.

Stem Stitch

Each stitch overlaps the previous stitch to one side, forming a twisted line. This stitch is often used for the vines and stems on floral designs, hence how it got its name.

1. From the wrong side bring your needle to the right side.

2. Dive your needle down a short ways away, in the direction you want your line to go.

3. Bring your needle up to the right, half way between the stitch just formed. Be careful to not nick into the original stitch.

4. Following your line, dive your needle down a short ways away.

5. Bring your needle up to the right side at the point where the stitch dove in (at the half way mark). Continue following steps 4 and 5.

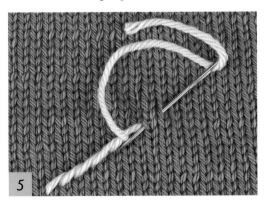

Straight Stitch

This is a single isolated stitch. It can be made any size, although do not make is so long as to catch on things easily. It is a quick stitch that can be used to fill in an area, or sporadically used, for example; whiskers in the cat motif.

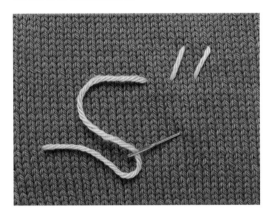

DECORATIVE EMBELLISHMENTS

Walk through any craft or fabric store to find a wealth of embellishment ideas. There are ribbons, lace, flowers, buttons, ric rac, braids, beads, the lists goes on. Look through these aisles and come up with ways to add embellishment to your knit projects and garments.

Embellishment Samples

EMBROIDERED FLOWERS

Simple star-shaped flowers will add pizzazz to any plain piece of knitting.
This design uses French knots, detached chain stitch, stem stitch, and a bit
of weaving.

Two colors: A and B

⊗ = French knots: Wrap needle twice for large flower; once for small flower

〰〰〰 = stem stitch

⬭ = detached chain stitch

With A, CO 37 sts.

Work St st for 48 rows, BO.

Following chart and with color B embroider flowers as charted.

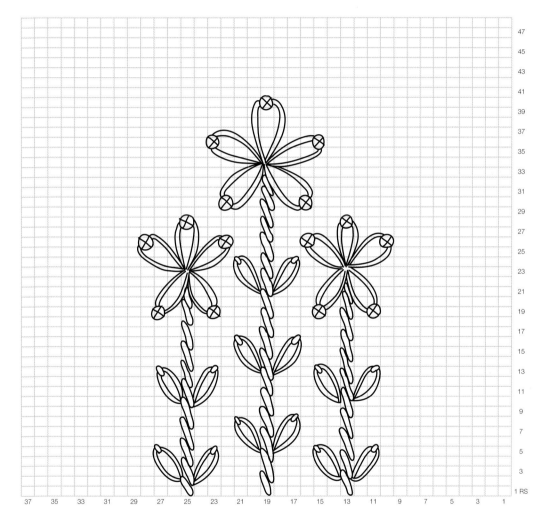

Flower Center Weaving

Weave in and out through flower petals; three times around for large flowers, twice around for small flowers.

RIBBON STRIPES

Purchased ribbon embellishes a basic stripe pattern. There are many different choices in ribbons, satin as used here, grosgrain, sheer, etc., giving many variations to the theme. This technique can be used as an afterthought embellishment, because the ribbon is pulled through the spaces within the stitches. However, if using a larger ribbon, a yarn over or a buttonhole would accommodate the ribbon better.

Two colors: A and B, plus ribbon.

With A, CO 43 stitches. Work in St st:
12 rows in color A
7 rows in color B
7 Rows in color A
7 rows in color B
12 rows in color A

When complete, weave ribbon using the photo as a guide.

VINES AND BUDS

Add delightful texture and detail to stranded knitting with detached chain stitch petals and French knot centers.

Multiple of 14 sts plus 1.
Three colors: A, B, and C.

■ = A
■ = B
☐ = C

X = With A, make three detached chain stitches for petals.
With B, make French knots in center, wrapping only once.

With C, CO 45 sts.
Using the stranded technique, knit 47 rows. Using chart as a guide, embroider two-colored flowers at X's.

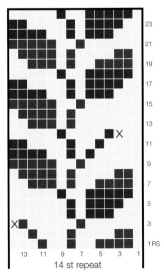

14 st repeat

FRUIT WITH EMBROIDERY

Simple intarsia knitting comes to life with embroidered French knot spots, detached chain stitch fruit topper, and stems stitched in appropriately named stem stitch.

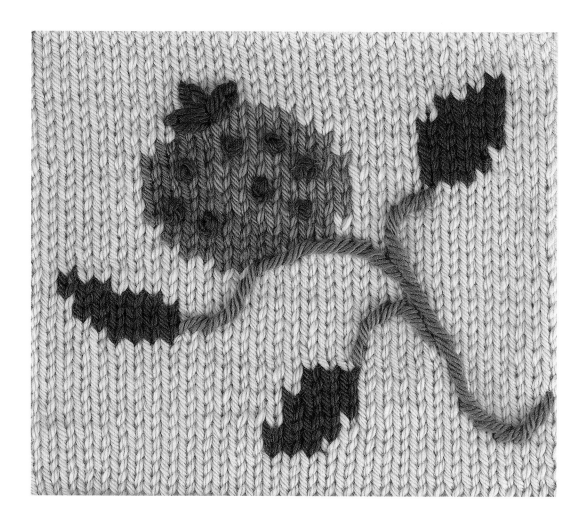

Five colors: A, B, C, D, and E.

With A, CO 33 sts.
Using the intarsia technique, work through row 40.
Using chart as guide, embroider details onto fruit.

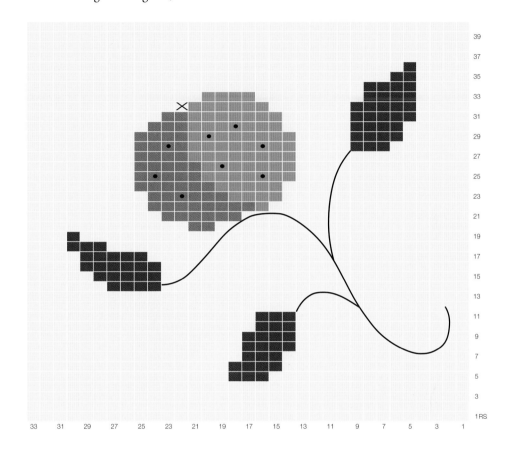

▨ = A
▨ = C
▨ = D
■ = B
● = With B: make French knots (wrap only once around needle)
✕ = With B: make 3 detatched chain stitches (Lazy Daisy)
⌐ = With E, work stem stitch

Embellished Mosaic Belt

A fun way to introduce color to a project is to add something unexpected. The use of cording from the fabric store is one such way. This belt is made using a simple mosaic stitch in two colors, and when finished, a cording is woven through and used to tie your belt around your waist or lower on your hips. Refer to page 31 for mosaic knitting techniques.

MATERIALS

1 each Berroco Vintage 50% Acrylic, 40% Wool, 10% Nylon; 3.5 oz (100 g), 217 yd (200 m) 51191 Blue (A), 5182 Dark Plum (B)

Size 7 (4.5 mm) needles or size to obtain gauge

4½ yards (4.2 m) cording

Gauge

17 sts = 2¾" (7 cm) in Mosaic stitch on size 7 (4.5 mm) needles

Finished Measurements

2¾" (7 cm) wide, 39" (99 cm) long not including the ties

Instructions

With A, Cable CO 5 sts. Refer to chart for shaping and color changes. This belt can be easily shortened or lengthened depending on how many repeats of the pattern are made. This belt has 11 repeats. Each repeat is approx. 2½" (6.5 cm). If you add length to your belt you will need to add length to the cording.

Finishing: Tape ends of cording as they will fray. Cut cording in half. The tape acts like the hard end of shoe lace and will aid in lacing cording through the stitches that are slipped. Refer to guide for lacing. When finished knot ends and cut off tape, and unravel to achieve fringe.

Embellished Mosaic Belt Chart

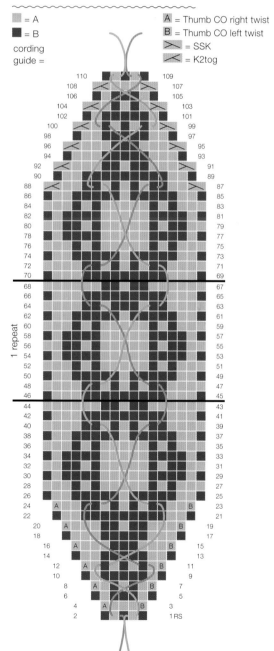

= A	
= B	
cording guide =	
A = Thumb CO right twist	
B = Thumb CO left twist	
= SSK	
= K2tog	

Slip Stitch Vest with Scarf

Lovely and vibrant alpaca yarn makes for a pleasing vest and scarf combination. The cropped vest is made with a bright three-color edging, scallops on the bottom edge, and picots on the neck and armhole boarders. The body of the sweater is made with a V-shaped two-color slip stitch pattern. The matching-color scarf is made with intarsia leaves and a different one-color slip stitch. The slip stitch mimics ribbing and will make the scarf lay nicely around your neck. One end of the scarf has the scallop edging and the other end is finished off with the picot edging.

MATERIALS

Shown: Frog Tree Alpaca Sport 100% Alpaca; 1.75 oz (50 g), 130 yd (118 m): 4 (5, 5, 6, 6) skeins 45 Dark Green (A), 3 (4, 4, 5, 5) skeins 41 Green (B), 1 skein each of 57 Fuchsia (C), 25 Rose (D), 501 Purple (E)

Size 3 (3.25 mm) 16" (41 cm) & 24" (61 cm) circular needle or size to obtain gauge

Size 4 (3.40 mm) 16" (41 cm) & 24"(61 cm) circular needles or size needed to obtain gauge

Size 5 (3.75 mm) 24" (61 cm) circular needle or size to obtain gauge

Markers (locking)

Holders

Tapestry Needle

Size

Small, Medium, Large, 1X, 2X (shown in size Small)

Finished Measurements

Vest

Bust: 38" (44", 48", 52", 56") 96.5 cm (112 cm, 122 cm, 132 cm, 142.5 cm)

Length: 20½" (21", 22", 23', 24") 52 cm (53.5 cm, 56 cm, 58.5 cm, 61 cm)

Scarf

5" (12.75 cm) end on Intarsia side, 4" (10 cm) end of Slip Stitch side by 32¾" (32 ¾", 33¾", 34¼", 35 ¼") 83.5 cm (83.5 cm, 86 cm, 89.5 cm)

Gauge

Vest: 28 sts and 30 rows = 4"(10 cm) in Slip Stitch pattern A on size 5 (3.75 mm) needles
Scarf: 24 sts and 32 rows = 4" (10 cm) in Stockinette Stitch and Intarsia on size 3 (3.25 mm) needles

Vest Slip Stitch Chart

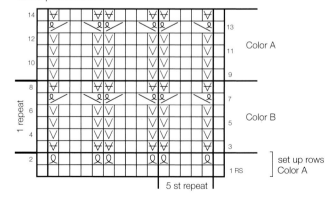

Repeat rows 3-14 for pattern

☐ = K on RS, P on WS

Ջ = wrap yarn twice around needle (row 2 only)

V = slip stitch

⩔ = slip stitch dropping one of the double wrap

⟍Ջ = Left Cross with Double Wrap:
Go under Sl st and K 2nd St wrapping twice Pull wraps through and insert needle into Sl st as if to p, take both sts off.

Ջ⟋ = Right Cross with Double Wrap:
Insert needle through Sl st and 1st st as if to K2 tog, wrap twice, *instead* of pulling double wrap through both sts put point of needle between sl st and 1st st, pull off needle.

Neck chart slip stitch vest

Sizes S and XXL

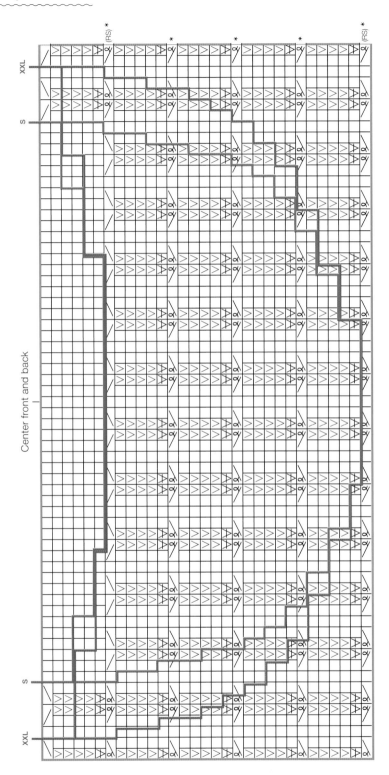

*This is a row 7 (color B) or a row 13 (color A) of the repeat. Cross your stitches but DO NOT double wrap if you cannot complete the repeat to the the next cross and double wrap. Otherwise, in your BO, you will have a long loop to deal with.

Sizes M, L, XL

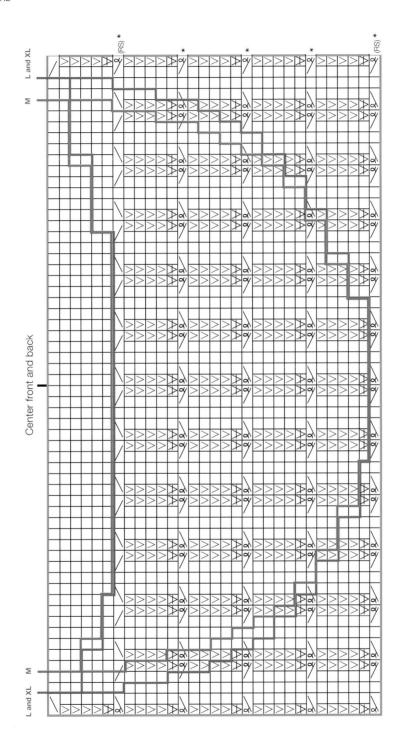

Scarf
Intarsia Chart

1) **I** = Inc by knitting into the front and back of st

2) • Background is dark green (A)

• Darkest chart color is fuchsia (C)

• Lightest chart color is rose (D)

3) Embroider stems and veins w/ 3 Strands of purple (E)

4) ⊟ = purl st (K on WS)

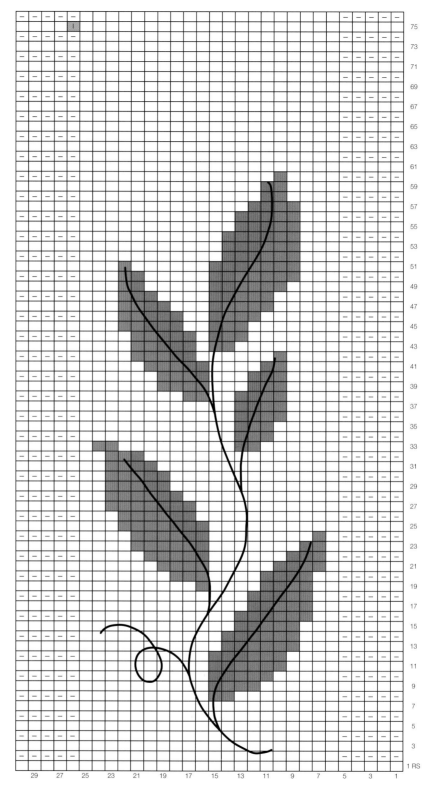

Scarf Slip Stitch Chart 2

Legend:
- Ω = wrap yarn twice around needle
- – = knit on WS
- ⋈ = Slip St dropping one of the double wraps
- V = Slip Stitch

Scallop Edging

Multiple of 9 sts plus 1
(at end of row 1: 2 sts plus 1 and at end of row 2: 4 sts plus 1)
Three colors: C, D and E.

With color C:
Row 1 (RS): *K1, k8, sl 7 sts over 1st; repeat from *, end k1.
Row 2: *P1, M1(by thumb method); repeat from *, end p1.
Rows 3 & 4: Knit.

Change to D:
Rows 5 & 6: Knit.
Row 7: *K2tog, yo; repeat from *, end k1.
Row 8: Knit.

Change to E:
Rows 9, 10: knit.

Picot BO

Multiple of 2 plus 2 edge sts

With color C
K2, pull 1st st over 2nd. * Put st back onto LH needle. Cable CO 2 sts. K3 sts, pass 2nd and 3rd over 1st st, BO 2 sts. Repeat from *.

Vest Back

With size 4 (3.50 mm) 24"(61 cm) needles and C, Cable CO 243 (270, 306, 324, 351) sts. Start Scallop Edging working pattern and color changes as indicated. After row 2, 108 (120, 136, 144, 156) sts remain. When row 10 is completed: knit evenly increasing 29 (32, 36, 38, 41) sts by knitting in the front and the back of the stitch for a total of 137 (152, 172, 182, 197) sts.

Change to size 5 (3.75 mm) 24" (61 cm) needles. Start Vest Slip Stitch Chart working pattern and color changes as indicated until back measures approximately 15" (15½", 16½", 17½", 18½") 38 cm (39.5 cm, 42 cm, 44.5 cm, 47 cm) ending on a row 6 or 12.

Back and Front Neck Shaping

Notes: A chart of the back and front neck shaping is included for a visual aid in determining where the shaping occurs within the Slip Stitch repeat. This is especially important for row 7 and 13 where a double wrap is made. When BO you do not want a double wrap because you would have a long loop to deal with. So on rows 7 and 13 only single wrap if you cannot complete the left or right cross 6 rows later.

The chart only represents the stitches closest to the neck line and does not include the shoulder area, therefore I have you place markers on the body to delineate these areas. Work outside the markers as established.

Back Neck

Place markers to represent the stitches within the Neck Chart: on right side count 36 (46, 56, 61, 66) sts, PM, center 65 (60, 60, 60, 65) sts, PM, and left side 36 (46, 56, 61, 66) sts. Next will be a row 7 or 13. Continue as established for color changes and patterning using neck chart to BO and shape back neck sts within markers (ignore front neck shaping).

Note: The chart has both the front and back BO markings, so when working the back you will work 4 slip stitch repeats (shown on chart) before you start making your back neck shaping.

On final row do not double wrap any of the shoulder stitches, wrap only once.

Next purl one row with established color and place 43 (50, 58, 62, 68) sts. Place live shoulder sts on holders.

Front

Make front exactly as back, and at neck use front neck shaping from the chart. Block pieces, then 3-needle BO shoulders together, RS facing in.

Armhole Edging

Place marker 11" (11", 12", 12", 12½") 28 cm (28 cm, 30.5 cm, 30.5 cm, 32 cm) down from shoulder seams on both the front and back. With size 4 (3.40 mm) needles and color E start at left front pick up 55 (55, 63, 63, 63) sts, pick up same amount along back for a total of 110 (110, 126, 126, 132) sts. Knit 3 rows (2 garter ridges).

Change to D.
Row 1: knit.
Row 2: knit and at the same time evenly dec 5 (5, 7, 7, 7) sts. 105 (105, 119, 119, 125) sts.
Row 3: *k2tog, yo; repeat from *, end k1
Row 4: knit.

Change to size 3 (3.25mm) needles and C.
Row 1: knit.
Row 2: knit and at the same time evenly dec 17 (17, 23, 23, 25). 88 (88, 96, 96, 100) sts.
Row 3: knit.
Next row (RS) work Picot BO.

Neck

The following instructions are very detailed to minimize the texture and color jog that can occur with circular knitting. Also refer to jog fixes on pages 14 and 15.

With size 4 (3.50 mm) 16" (41 cm) needle and E, beginning at back evenly pick up 45 (47, 49, 49, 55) sts, along front evenly pick up 67 (67, 73, 73, 79) sts, for a total of 112 (112, 122, 122, 134) sts. Next join, purling around neck. Next slip first st after marker. Knit around neck plus the slip st after marker. Slip next st (your now at 2 sts past marker) and purl around neck plus 2 slip sts after marker. Cut yarn and slide 2 sl sts back to LH needle.

With D
Row 1: knit.
Row 2: purl and at the same time evenly dec 22 (22, 24, 24, 26) sts, for a total of 90 (90, 98, 98, 108) sts, slip next st.
Row 3 Next *K2tog, yo; repeat from *. Slip next st (your now 2 sts past marker)
Row 4: Purl around neck plus 2 sts past marker.
Cut yarn and slide 2 sl stitches back to LH needle.

Change to size 3 (3.25 mm) needle and C.
Row 1: knit.
Row 2: purl and at the same time evenly dec 22 (22, 24, 24, 26) sts, for a total of 68 (68, 74, 74, 82) sts, slip next st.
Row 3: Knit 1 row plus the slip st.
Next row work Picot BO.

Finish
Sew side seams and under arm edging.

Scarf

With size 4 (3.50 mm) needles and C, Cable CO 55 sts. Follow Scallop Edging for color changes and pattern rows 1-10, ignoring stitch counts.
At the end of row 2 you should have 25 sts, (6 scallops plus one st).

Row 11: Evenly inc 5 sts by knitting into the front and back of st, 30 sts.

Change to size 3 (3.25 mm) needles and follow Intarsia Scarf chart through row 76. Next follow Scarf Slip Stitch chart B until piece measures 31½" (80 cm), ending on a WS row 2, but do not double wrap on previous row 1.

Final Edging

Change to size 4 (3.50 mm) needles and E.
Row 1: knit and evenly decrease 9 sts. (21sts)
Rows 2, 3 and 4 k (2 garter ridges)

Change to D
Row 1: knit.
Row 2: k and evenly decrease 2 sts. (19sts)
Row 3: *k2tog, yo; repeat from *, end k1.
Row 4: knit.

Change to size 3 (3.25mm) needles and C
Row 1: knit.
Row 2: knit and evenly decrease 3 sts. (16sts)
Row 3: knit.
Row 4: work Picot BO.

Embroider stems and veins with 3 strands of E.

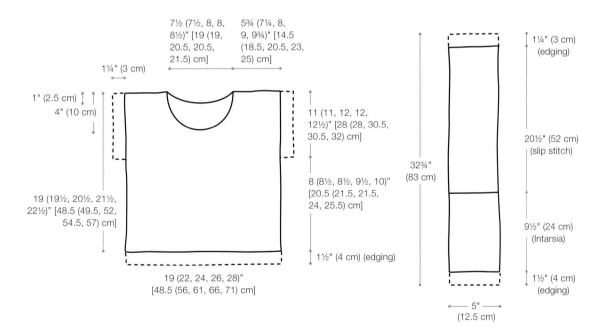

Embellished Butterfly Purse

Everyone needs a small purse, and this one is decorated with an intarsia butterfly, a braided strap, and a long fringe. To simplify the knitting, duplicate stitch the butterfly's outline. The purse is knit in one piece, folded in half and the side seams are sewn. A line of purl stitches at the fold line makes it easy to attach fringe on the bottom.

MATERIALS

Shown: Louet Gems #2 Fine/Sport Weight Wool 100% Merino Wool; 1.35 oz (100 g), 225 yd (205 m): 1 skein each 66 Bright Blue (A), 65 Golden Rod (B), 05 Goldilocks (C), scrap of Dark Blue (D)

Size 3 (3.25 mm) needles or size to obtain gauge

Size 4 (3.50 mm) needles or size to obtain gauge

Small crochet hook

Gauge

24 sts and 36 rows = 4" (10 cm) in Stockinette Stitch on size 4 (3.25 mm) needles

Finished Measurements

5" (13 cm) wide by 4¼" (11 cm) long (not including fringe)

Purse Body

With A, Cable CO 33 sts.

Work in Stockinette Stitch.

Follow chart, changing needle sizes as indicated and work butterfly motif using the intarsia technique. To make the intarsia knitting easier duplicate stitch color D, the outline around the butterfly.

Block.

Sew up side seams.

Strap

Cut 6 lengths of color A, 1⅞ yds (1.73 m) long. Holding the 6 strands together, knot one end and pin or tape down. Braid two strands in each section the entire length and knot. When finished, machine sew the ends so they will lay flat and cut off knots. A knot will add too much bulk. Whip stitch at least 1" (2.5 cm) of braid to side seams of purse.

Fringe

Cut 30 lengths of color A, 11" (28 cm) long. Using a small crochet hook, insert through center purl bump from back to front. Fold 2 pieces of cut fringe in half, using crochet hook pull through purl bump and make a loop. Place ends through loop and tighten. One fringe made. Continue along one side making the fringe in every other purl bump. Finish other side, 15 fringes total. Trim fringes even.

Embellished Butterfly Purse Chart

Use size 3 needles

= W/A, K on RS, P on WS

– = W/A, K on WS

Use size 4 needles

= A bright blue

= B golden rod

= C goldilocks

= D dark blue

Knitting Techniques

CABLE CAST ON

A wonderful cast on is the Cable cast on. It is decorative and stretchy.

1. Place a slip knot on your left-hand needle. Insert right hand needle into slip knot as if to knit, pull stitch through and place on left-hand needle.

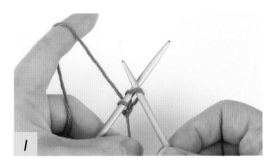

2. Next * insert right-hand needle between stitches, wrap yarn, pull stitch through and place on left-hand needle *, repeat from * to end.

Tip: When using a cable cast on, the first two stitches are a slip knot and knitting into the slip knot, which looks different from the rest of the

stitches. Cast on two extra stitches. On your first row of knitting, drop the last two stitches (the slip knot and knitting into the slip knot stitches).

They will unravel without picking the stitches apart and now all the stitches left on the needle look the same. You can use this for flat knitting or for circular knitting. If circular knitting, this area will graft nicely together.

Tip: When working in the round, knit one row flat and then join the knitting. This makes it easier to see if any stitches are getting twisted around the needle. When the garment or project is finished, you can neatly close the opening, matching the slant of the decorative edge. This also works well if you need to put your work on double pointed needles. First cable cast onto a circular needle (any length), knit your first row onto your double pointed needles, evenly spacing your stitches. Join in the next row. This makes it easy to see if any stitches became twisted and will make a neat closure when finishing your project.

PROVISIONAL CAST ON (CROCHETED)

Use this cast on when you want live stitches to work with later. For example, at the bottom of a purse where you will work one side and later go back and work the other side.

1. Using waste yarn, make a slip knot on your crochet hook, leave it on the hook.

2. Hold your knitting needle with the yarn under it and the crochet hook over your needle.

3. Wrap yarn with the hook and pull through.

4. Slide the yarn between the needle and hook, and then around to the back of the needle again.

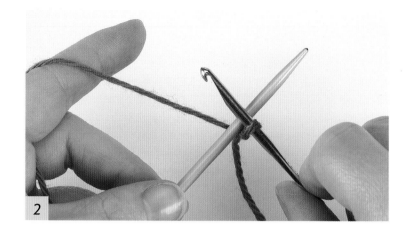

Continue with steps 3 and 4 until you have enough stitches. With your hook only, chain 2 or 3 more stitches. Cut yarn and pull tail through. Chaining two or three extra stitches at the end will make it easy to see which end to unravel when ready to pick up and knit the other way.

Note: when you unravel and pick up your stitches you will be one stitch short, so increase one stitch.

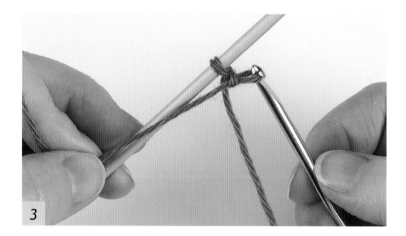

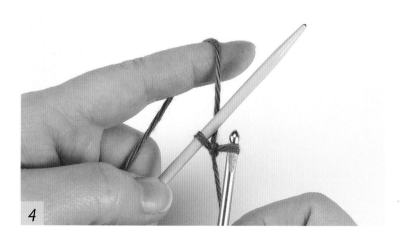

THUMB CAST ON
OR INCREASE

▲ Thumb Cast On Right Twist

Right Twist

Start with a slip knot on your right hand needle. To make a twist to the right, twirl yarn around thumb from outside in, insert needle upward through loop and pull off thumb, which makes a twist to the right.

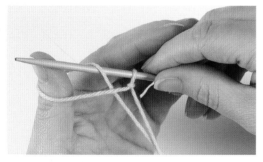

▲ Thumb Cast On Left Twist

Left Twist

Start with a slip knot on your right-hand needle. To make a twist to the left, wrap yarn opposite way, inside out, around thumb, insert needle upward through loop made. Pull off thumb.

THREE-NEEDLE BIND OFF

This bind off is typically used to attach shoulder seams, but in this book it is also used to close pillows, and join the top of a hat.

1. Place stitches to be joined on separate needles.
2. Hold needles right sides together.
3. Using a third needle Insert into first stitches of

both needles.
4. Wrap yarn around and pull through both stitches.
5. Slip the stitches off left needles.
Repeat steps 1-5 once more. Two stitches are on your right hand needle. Bind off the first stitch by passing it over the second. Continue in this manner to 3 needle bind off.

I-CORD

Use double pointed needles as you will not turn your work but slide your stitches back to the start/other end of the needle.

1. Cast on 3 sts (or whatever your pattern calls for).
2. Knit 3 stitches.
3. Slip the stitches to the other end of needle, and knit these 3 stitches again.
You will see the working yarn angle across the back. Repeat row 3, and a tube will start forming. Work to your desired length.

TWISTED CORD

To make a twisted cord:

1. Figure out the length you need and cut yarn 3 times that length.
2. Tie a knot on each end.
3. Fasten one end. Have someone hold it for you, or securely tape it down.
4. Slip the other knotted end over a pencil (or a knitting needle) and twist.
Twist until cord folds back upon itself. Bring two ends together and knot. Run your fingers over the cord to smooth it out.

KNITTING TERMS & ABBREVIATIONS

approx	approximate		p	purl
beg	begin(ning)		p2tog	purl two together
BO	bind off		PM	place marker
CC	contrasting color		psso	past slip stitch over
CO	cast on		PU	pick up
cont	continue		RF	right front
dec	decrease		rem	remaining
dpn	double-pointed needles		RS	right side
inc	increase		sl	slip
k	knit		sl m	slip marker
k2tog	knit two together		ssk	slip, slip, knit two stitches together
k2tog tbl	knit two together through back loops		st(s)	stitch(es)
LF	left front		St st	stockinette stitch
M1	make one		tog	together
M2	make two		WS	wrong side
MC	main color		wyib	with yarn in back
m	meter		wyif	with yarn in front
			yo	yarn over

YARN RESOURCES

Berroco Yarns
PO Box 367
Uxbridge, MA 01569-0367
www.berroco.com

Blue Sky Alpacas, Inc
PO Box 88
Cedar, MN 55011
www.blueskyalpacas.com

Brown Sheep Co., Inc
100662 County Road 16
Mitchell, NE 69357
www.brownsheep.com

Frog Tree Alpacas
T & C Imports
PO Box 1119
East Dennis, MA 02641
www.frogtreeyarns.com

Louet North America
808 Commerce Park Drive
Ogdensburg, NY 13669
www.louet.com

Rauma Yarns
Nordic Fiber Arts
4 Cutts Road
Durham, NH 03824
www.nordicfiberarts.com

Shibui Knits
1500 NW 18th Suite 110
Portland, OR 97209
www.shibuiknits.com

REFERENCE BOOKS

Allen, Pam. *Knitting for Dummies*. New York, NY: Hungry Minds, 2002.

Bourgeois, Ann, and Eugene Bourgeois. *Fair Isle Sweaters Simplified*. Bothell, WA: Martingale & Company, 2000.

Carroll, Amy, ed. *Pattern Library: Knitting*. New York: Ballantine, 1981.

Feitelson, Ann. *The Art of Fair Isle Knitting: History, Technique, Color & Patterns*. Loveland, CO: Interweave, 1996.

Gravelle, LeCount Cynthia., and Loren McIntyre. *Andean Folk Knitting*. Saint Paul, MN: Dos Tejedoras Fiber Arts Publications, 1990.

Harrell, Betsy. *Anatolian Knitting Designs: Sivas Stocking Patterns*. Istanbul, Türkiye: Redhouse, 1981.

Hiatt, June. *The Principles of Knitting: Methods and Techniques of Hand Knitting*. New York: Simon and Schuster, 1988.

Ihnen, Lori. *A Garden Stroll: Knits Inspired by Nature*. Woodinville, WA: Martingale, 2004.

McGregor, Sheila. *Traditional Fair Isle Knitting*. New York: Dover Publications, 2003.

McGregor, Sheila. *Traditional Scandinavian Knitting*. Mineola, NY: Dover Publications, 2004.

Radcliffe, Margaret. *The Essential Guide to Color Knitting Technique*. North Adams, MA: Storey, 2008.

Starmore, Alice. *Alice Starmore's Book of Fair Isle Knitting*. Newtown, CT: Taunton, 1988.

Stuever, Sherry, and Keely Stuever. *Intarsia, A Workshop for Hand & Machine Knitting*. Guthrie, OK: Sealed With A Kiss, 1998.

The Harmony Guides Knitting Techniques: All You Need to Know about Hand Knitting, Volume 1. London: Collins & Brown, 1998.

Thomas, Mary. *Mary Thomas's Book of Knitting Patterns*. New York: Dover, 1972.

Thomas, Mary. *Mary Thomas's Knitting Book*. New York: Dover Publications, 1972.

Walker, Barbara G. *Charted Knitting Designs*. New York: Scribner, 1972.

Williams, Joyce, Meg Swansen, and Amy Detjen. *Sweaters from Camp: 38 Color-patterned Designs from Meg Swansen's Knitting Campers*. Pittsville, WI: Schoolhouse, 2002.

INDEX